EXPLORING SPACE

Using Seymour Simon's Astronomy Books in the Classroom

Barbara Bourne · Wendy Saul

MORROW JUNIOR BOOKS · New York

We dedicate this book to the many teachers with whom we work and from whom we learn.

ACKNOWLEDGMENTS

We wish to thank David Reuther of Morrow Junior Books for recognizing the need to build curriculum from excellent nonfiction and inviting us to write this book. Thanks also to Michael Street for his careful editorial assistance. Seymour Simon has been both a literary inspiration and a friend of this project. We thank him not only for his obvious help with this book, but also for his valuing of teacher knowledge.

The Elementary Science Integration Project (ESIP), a consortium of classroom teachers and their students who seek science opportunities across the curriculum, fundamentally shapes our sense of audience. Several ESIP teachers—Susan Wells, Charles Pearce, Debra Bunn, Rob Piper, and Maureen Hoyer—played a special role this time. Their activities and comments breathed life into this book.

We also wish to acknowledge the help of the National Science Foundation for its support of ESIP.

The material in this volume is based upon work supported in part by the National Science Foundation under grant number TPE-8955187. Any opinions, findings, and conclusions or recommendations expressed in this material are those of the authors and do not necessarily reflect the views of the National Science Foundation.

Library of Congress Cataloging-in-Publication Data
Bourne, Barbara.
    Exploring space: using Seymour Simon's astronomy books in the classroom/Barbara Bourne, Wendy Saul.
        p.   cm.
        ISBN 0-688-13643-5
    1. Astronomy—Study and teaching—Activity programs. 2. Outer space—Study and teaching. I. Saul, Wendy. II. Title. QB61.B68 1994
520—dc20   93-51249   CIP

Photo and Art Credits
Permission to use the following photographs is gratefully acknowledged: pages 1, 4, 6, 9, 13, 25, 33, 37, 43 (left), 51, 53, 57, 75, 83, and 85, NASA; pages 19, 27, 39, 43 (right), 45, 71, and 89, Jet Propulsion Laboratory (California Institute of Technology)/NASA; pages 55, 67, 77, and 87, National Optical Astronomy Observatories.

Illustrations on pages 23, 29, 31, 41, 47, 59, 61, 63, and 65 by Ann Neumann; on page 49 by Frank Schwarz; and on page 79 by Warren Budd.

Contents

A Message from Seymour Simon

The universe is full of wonderful things for us to discover. I felt that way when I was a child reading science-fiction stories about imaginary trips to the stars, and I still feel that way when I read true science accounts of space probes visiting Mars or when I look at a photo of a distant galaxy or a close-up view of an asteroid.

I try to communicate that same sense of excitement when I write books about space, and I also tried to when I taught science in public school. To my mind, science is never bor-r-ring! So I did all the things that I could think of to make science fun, interesting, and understandable for the children in my classes. What I would have given to have had a book like this to help me when I was teaching! (I'm also a little chagrined that I didn't think of many of these ideas myself.)

Barbara Bourne and Wendy Saul have used my books about outer space as a launching pad to explore all kinds of creative adventures with children. The imaginative activities range from hands-on experiments and investigations to using language, art, and library skills to working on interpersonal relations and individual development ideas. Above all, their ideas make learning and science fun and not the dreaded *b* word.

What's also wonderful about this book is that its use is not restricted to just one set of subject books by one author. Barbara and Wendy frequently cite other books and other authors, and I can easily imagine this book serving as a source of ideas and a model for teaching any subject, not just space. I am pleased and proud to be associated with this unique guide for teachers and parents.

A star cluster.

Readers' Quiz

- Are you interested in space science, and do you want to find ways to share that interest with young people?
- Are you the kind of teacher, parent, or librarian who builds on children's curiosities and recognizes that most kids are intrigued by astronomy?
- Does astronomy loom large in your program of study?
- Are you and your students looking to find ways to extend Seymour Simon's books with related activities?
- Are you interested in ways to integrate your curriculum, to teach science with reading and language arts and mathematics?
- Do you see hands-on science as an effective and exciting way to help kids make sense of the physical world?
- Are you looking for ways to extend hands-on science across the curriculum?
- Are you looking for something to do tomorrow? For the next week? For activities that thread throughout the entire year?

If the answer to any one of these questions is yes, then this book is for you.

How to Use This Book

The following icons are used throughout the book:

 You Will Need

You will be given a list of materials needed to complete each activity. Gather them *before* you begin.

Most materials should be available at your school. Read through the list a day in advance in case there is something you or your students need to bring from home.

Often the list will include books on a given topic. Although this activity guide was written to complement books by Seymour Simon, there are many excellent books by other authors. Feel free to use them.

 Procedure

This section explains how to carry out the activity. Read through it in advance so you will be prepared for each step.

 Digging Deeper

After completing an activity, some children want to do more. This section includes ideas to continue an activity, suggestions for further reading, and topics for class discussions.

 In Your Journal

Keeping a journal is an important way to record thoughts. Read through the **Astronomy Journals** activity (page 12) to help set up your students' journals.

 Read More about It

In **Read More about It,** you will find suggestions for uncovering more in the books around you.

These ideas are designed to help you establish closer science-literature connections. Find your own books and encourage students to read them in their own ways.

 Seymour Says

Read Seymour Simon's own words about writing, science, and astronomy. They serve as a good model for would-be scientists and writers.

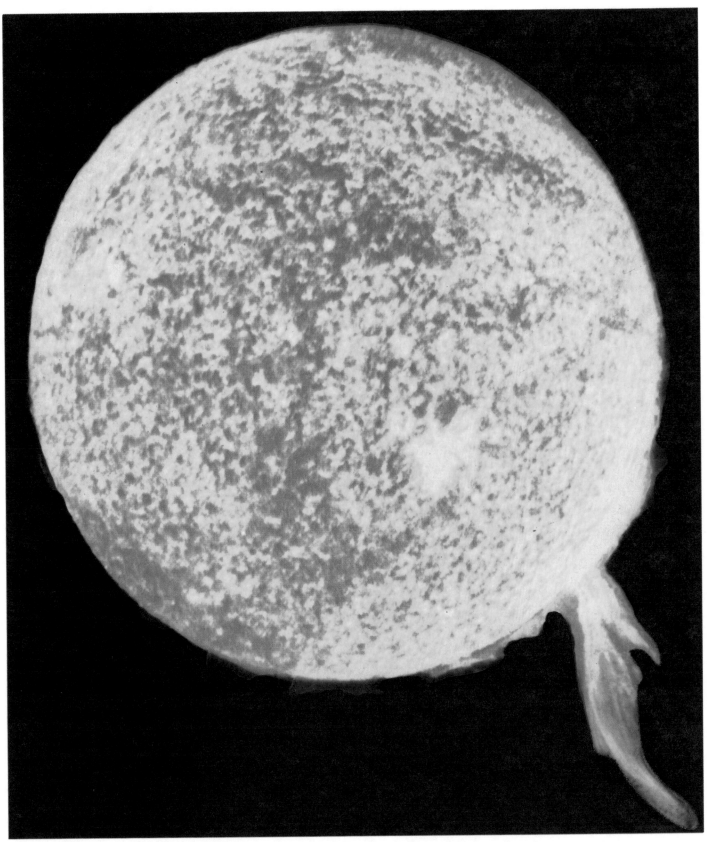

The Sun is nearly six hundred times bigger than all the planets in the Solar System combined.

Where to Begin

In the days of workbooks the teacher's job was different. He or she would direct students to turn to the appropriate page, spend twenty minutes filling in the blanks, and submit their completed work sheets. A gold star signaled complete success. Children were chastised for moving ahead without permission, and proceeding too fast or too slowly was strictly forbidden. Learning was like walking a balance beam—it was a narrow ridge, and children were always in danger of falling off. The irony, of course, is that lifelong learning strategies—problem solving, persistence, decision making—were either ignored or squelched.

Educators who identify with constructivist and whole language approaches—in other words, approaches that are meaning-centered—have taken a markedly different view of both teacher and student. They recognize that children profit from knowing as much as possible about what James Rutherford, chief education officer of the American Association for the Advancement of Science, calls the intellectual "neighborhood" in which they operate.

We encourage you to view the study of astronomy as a journey. Leave room for investigative side trips. Give your students time to get their bearings. Encourage them to wander the territory you will soon explore together.

What might such explorations look like in a classroom? What might a teacher do to encourage a broad, integrated look at astronomy? With these questions in mind, we followed three teachers as they guided their students through an exploration of astronomy and some of Seymour Simon's books.

Charles Pearce started by attaching the study of space to class work undertaken on Earth science. He began with the purpose of comparing Earth to other planets: "Suppose we were a publishing company and we hired an author to write a series of books about the Solar System. What would we want these books to look like? What facts should be included? What questions should be answered? What type of illustrations should we use?"

In the ensuing discussion, student interest leapfrogged across topics: atmosphere to ozone to planet temperatures to gravity to life on other planets to space travel. Mr. Pearce recorded students' questions and then moved on. "It appears that one author has already prepared such a series," he began, slowly pulling books one by one from a newly opened box. "Let's take a look at these." Singly and in small groups students enthusiastically chose titles to explore: *The Sun, Saturn, Mars, Venus*...

Twenty minutes later Mr. Pearce drew the children together. They were eager to share what they had discovered—ready to work, ready to learn, ready to search for answers to questions they had asked themselves.

Susan Wells, another teacher committed to helping students check out the neighborhood of science before beginning specific investigations, started her class off with a tease, a short booktalk focusing on illustrations from Seymour Simon's *The Sun*. The students then used **Know, Wonder, Learn** charts (see page 14) to record what they already knew and what they wondered about the Sun. Later they would return to the chart, answering, correcting, and adding to their notions and questions with what they had learned from their reading. This strategy allowed the teacher to sense particular areas of student strengths and interests, as well as identify gaps in student knowledge.

Finally Ms. Wells offered her children a challenge: "Pretend that Seymour Simon's publisher asked you to write and illustrate one more page for *The Sun*. What information would you add?"

Because Ms. Wells had collected multiple copies of this particular volume, students were able to compare and contrast their ideas and findings. A similar procedure could be developed by issuing the same challenge to groups using different volumes from the astronomy series. After more than a full hour of intense classroom activity—researching other texts, writing, illustrating, editing—students gathered to share their ideas. The stage was set for study.

Debra Bunn approached the books through hands-on activities. Because her students were already familiar with Seymour Simon's astronomy series, she asked them to consider what investigations *they* might plan to help other students learn about the Solar System.

After forty minutes of browsing and developing projects, students shared their suggestions. Ms. Bunn listened carefully for ideas the children found most intriguing, for misconceptions, for the relationship between background knowledge, student reading, and persistent questions.

Although each of these teachers moved away from the confining, scripted learning procedures developed by basal publishers, it is important to note that each moved away in a different direction. They responded to the interests of the children in their charge, built on their own concerns and curiosities, and personalized public information.

Such is our hope for this book. In it you will find more ideas for activities than you have the time or interest to pursue in any given year. Pick and choose those you feel will be the most valuable. Take these ideas and make them your own. Invite children to amend and refine them. Let group activities become individual projects. Encourage students to build upon one another's work, in class, between classes, from one year to the next. Replace balance-beam teaching with forms that encourage inquiry, persistence, and meaningful work.

Some Other Bits of Advice

1. Each student does not need to engage in every activity. Encourage children to work in groups and individually, and to present their findings to the rest of the class.

2. Make friends with your librarian. There are a number of literature-based activities in this guide. Encourage students to participate in these activities by having relevant books available and displayed with the cover, not the spine, facing out.

3. Try not to rush students. If they wish to repeat an activity, let them. Sometimes they need time to worry ideas into place. We would be horrified to hear a teacher tell a youngster not to reread a piece of literature. Why don't we encourage a similar immersion in science?

4. Whenever possible, give students choices. There are plenty of activities available in this book. There are many more in resources listed in the bibliography. Students feel more invested in their studies if they are invited to "own" the ideas they have gathered.

5. Whenever possible, treat the class as a community of scientists engaged in collecting and analyzing data. Teacher questions focused on what students know are less productive than metacognitive questions on *how* they know, *when* they know, and *what* they can do to find out more.

6. Don't stop here. Use the activities in this guide as a model for science and language connections throughout your curriculum.

Astronomy Journals

Set up a place to record your thoughts and questions on the astronomy topics that interest you.

✔ YOU WILL NEED

- ☐ a three-ring binder
- ☐ dividers
- ☐ a three-hole pocket folder
- ☐ paper and a pencil

You can make an astronomy journal from any notebook, but try a three-ring binder so you can add new pages, graphs, charts, photos, and photocopies; rearrange pages; or even remove them temporarily.

Choose a sturdy binder, then add dividers so you will have sections in your journal, such as:

- **Research notes.** Are you conducting ongoing experiments? Keeping track of the constellations you find in the sky? Use one section for notes on research and long-term activities.
- **Questions.** As scientists read, research, and communicate with others, they develop new questions. Add your questions to this section as soon as they arise.
- **Amazing facts.** Keep a list of interesting facts that you find in your reading, discussions, and activities.
- **Book list.** Record the science books you are reading. Include title, author, and a brief description or review of the book.
- **Dialogue.** Maybe you have ideas you want to share with another scientist, or questions to which you can't find an answer. Use this section to communicate with a classmate or teacher. (Three-hole pocket folders will fit into your binder and can easily be removed for journal exchange.)
- **Just for me.** Scientists are not always ready to share their questions and research. Set up a section for *your* personal thoughts, questions, and theories. Move these pages to another section when you are ready to share them.
- **Special topic.** If you have one topic of particular interest (comets, black holes, Pluto), set aside a special section of your journal to record interesting facts, questions, or good books for future reference.
- **Exploring space.** Use this section for the **In Your Journal** activities from this book.

Saturn, the second largest planet after Jupiter.

Know, Wonder, Learn

Before you read a book, write down what you already know and what you wonder about the subject. As you read, add to your list of questions and write some of the new facts you have learned.

Title _____

Author _____

Subject _____

KNOW What do you know before you read?	WONDER What do you wonder about this subject?	LEARN What have you learned?

Astronomy Book Reviews

Complete this form and add to a class binder.

Title _____

Author _____

Date of publication _____ Number of pages _____

Book reviewer (your name) _____

Book topic _____

One word to describe this book is _____

This book is similar to (title/author) _____

Comment on the following book elements:

This book was _____ **easy** _____ **average** _____ **difficult** to read.

The author used _____ **humor** _____ **amazing facts** _____ **stories**

_____ **analogies and comparisons** _____ **questions** to keep the reader's attention.

The author _____ **always** _____ **usually** _____ **never** explained difficult concepts.

There are _____ **many** _____ **a few** _____ **no** illustrations.

The illustrations are _____ **black-and-white** _____ **color** _____ **drawings** _____ **photographs.**

Write one question to which you found an answer, or make up a riddle that can be answered, by reading this book.

_____

_____

The _____ **best** _____ **worst** thing about this book is _____

_____

I would recommend this book (check all that apply):

_____ for pleasure reading   _____ for research

_____ because of the illustrations _____ because of the author's writing

_____ for a younger child   _____ for an older student

_____ to my teacher   _____ other

Community Knowledge

Sharing information helps build a community of knowledge. Use this page to record interesting information you have uncovered in books or discovered in your activities. Record how you made this discovery by listing title, author, and page number, or details of the activity. Record any new questions you have—perhaps someone else has an idea. Add these pages to a class binder.

DATE	TOPIC	FACT	HOW/WHERE THIS WAS UNCOVERED	MY NEW QUESTIONS

Bridging the Gap

How do science writers make facts and figures real to their readers?

You Will Need

☐ astronomy books

Procedure

Authors use many language tools to help their readers understand abstract ideas. Here are some of the tools Seymour Simon uses to write his books.

- Comparisons: "If Earth were hollow, seven planets the size of Mars could fit inside." *(Mars)*
- References to everyday objects: Venus is "hotter than a kitchen oven set to broiling temperature." *(Venus)*
- Visual images: "If Pluto's orbit were the size of a quarter, the Oort cloud would be a giant, 50-foot-wide beach ball." *(Comets, Meteors, and Asteroids)*

1. Look through several astronomy books for phrases that help you picture a difficult idea or fact (such as size, temperature, speed).

2. Copy and illustrate one example.

3. Combine your paper with others in the class to make a book or bulletin board.

4. Write your own book about planets, stars, comets, meteors, or asteroids. Choose a special audience—students in a younger grade, your parents, or a school science club. As you write, think about what facts will be difficult for your readers to understand, then think of comparisons that would make the facts easier for these readers.

Digging Deeper

Set up a mini library of astronomy books on a table or bookshelf in your room. How do different authors treat the same subject? Which are you more likely to pick up for pleasure reading, for research, or for when you have only ten minutes to browse?

Include a variety of book genres on your shelf, along with a binder of book reviews (**Astronomy Book Reviews,** page 15).

- nonfiction, such as books by Seymour Simon, Isaac Asimov, Franklyn M. Branley, or Patricia Lauber
- poetry, such as *Space Songs*, by Myra Cohn Livingston
- science humor, such as the Magic School Bus books, by Joanna Cole
- science fiction
- activity and project books
- magazines, such as *Odyssey, Discover,* or *Astronomy*

Set up an author's table displaying several books by one author. How does that author adjust his or her writing to suit different purposes? A Seymour Simon astronomy table might include:

- *Comets, Meteors, and Asteroids; Mars; Stars; Venus;* and the others in this series
- *The Long View into Space* (Crown, 1979)
- collections of Einstein Anderson stories
- *Space Words* (HarperCollins, 1991)
- *Earth: Our Planet in Space; The Moon* (Four Winds/Macmillan, 1984)
- *Look to the Night Sky* (Puffin, 1979)

In Your Journal

Can you imagine using the words *not as hot* to describe something that is 10,000 degrees Fahrenheit? Would you describe an object that was 200 million years old as "young"? That's what Seymour Simon did when he wrote *Stars.*

What would you conclude about other stars in the Galaxy when you read that 200 million years old is "young" or 10,000 degrees is "not as hot"?

Questions, Facts, and Theories

Astronomy books are great resources for facts and theories about planets, stars, comets, meteors, and asteroids, but if you are like most scientists, the information you read will lead to more and more questions. Try this activity to keep track of where your questions lead.

YOU WILL NEED

- ☐ astronomy books such as Seymour Simon's *Our Solar System; Stars; Comets, Meteors, and Asteroids;* or books on any of the planets
- ☐ sentence strips
- ☐ yellow and blue index cards
- ☐ thumbtacks
- ☐ a bulletin board

PROCEDURE

1. Browse through some of the astronomy books in your classroom or library. You can read the text straight through or use the pictures to find parts that are interesting to you.

- What pictures or facts do you find interesting?
- What questions come to mind?
- Can you find the answers in the text?

2. Share one of your questions with at least two classmates. Maybe they have found an answer in one of their books. Perhaps you know the answer to a question of theirs.

3. Choose at least one of your questions. Write it on a sentence strip and hang it on the bulletin board.

4. Leave a supply of yellow and blue cards near the bulletin board for answers and theories.

5. If you have a hypothesis or theory about someone's question, write it on a yellow card and hang it under the sentence strip.

6. If you know a fact that can help answer a question, write it on a blue card and hang it under the sentence strip. (If that fact came from a book, be sure to include the title, author, and page number, so your classmates can read more.)

7. Keep track of your questions, facts, and theories. Some theories and facts may raise new questions. Make sure to add them to your question board.

DIGGING DEEPER

Is it important for scientists to completely answer one question before they move on to new questions?

IN YOUR JOURNAL

Make a question web in your journal. Write one question (from your class list or one of your own) at the center of the page. To complete your web, record some of the facts you would need to find an answer to this question. On the back of the page, make a list of resources (books, experts, museums, and so on) you could turn to for help.

READ MORE ABOUT IT

There are a number of books in your library that use a question-and-answer format. Roy Gallant's *101 Questions about the Universe* (Macmillan, 1984) focuses on space, but a book like Joanne Settel and Nancy Baggett's *Why Do Cats' Eyes Glow in the Dark?* (Atheneum, 1988), which centers on animal questions, can be just as effective for examining how question-and-answer books work. See if you and your friends can create your own question-and-answer book about an astronomy topic that interests you.

Olympus Mons on Mars, the largest known volcano on any planet in the Solar System.

This Week in Space

Bring a bit of space to Earth each week by sharing a book, conducting a game, or stumping the class with questions of the day.

✔ YOU WILL NEED

- ☐ the pages from this activity reproduced
- ☐ scissors
- ☐ index cards
- ☐ rubber cement
- ☐ a file box

➡ PROCEDURE

1. As a class, make one **This Week in Space** box.

   - Reproduce and cut out the activities on this page.
   - Glue each activity onto an index card. The paper will not wrinkle if you use rubber cement.

SPACE WORDS

Start or add to a class dictionary of astronomy vocabulary. Try to contribute at least five new words.

WHAT AM I?

Write at least five riddles about your topic. Add clues until someone gives the answer.

DESIGN A SPACE BULLETIN BOARD

Choose a theme for your bulletin board. Make the board colorful and informative. Leave room for your classmates' work to be added over the course of the week.

MATH MADNESS

Write three math story problems that use real data about your topic. Share them with your class.

HIS-STORY/HER-STORY

Write a brief biography of a scientist involved with your topic. Read it to the class, then add it to your class library.

QUESTIONS, PLEASE

Give your classmates a question of the day each morning. Provide resources they can use to answer it.

- Store the activities in your file box (you may want to decorate the box first).
- Keep the box where everyone can use it to plan activities for the class.

2. With a group, with a partner, or on your own, research a space topic: a planet; the Sun; stars; comets, meteors, and asteroids.

3. Use the activities stored in your **This Week in Space** box to organize a unit about your topic. Activities should be fun and informative.

4. After you have conducted an activity, write comments on the back of the card for the next person who uses it. List your name, topic, and suggestions for doing this activity another time. Return the card to the box.

5. You are not limited to the activity suggestions on these pages. Design your own activity. Write it on an index card and file it in the box.

6. As a class, decide if there are any activities *everybody* should include (such as adding to the mini space museum).

READ ALOUD

Read one of your favorite books aloud. Read several pages from an interesting book to your class or the children in a younger grade.

FIELD TRIP

Develop an in-school field trip. Take your classmates on an imaginary exploration of your planet, ride on your comet, or take a trip through your galaxy.

SPACE GAMES

Design, construct, and lead a game that helps students learn more about your space topic.

MINI SPACE MUSEUM

Add to a classroom mini space museum. Exhibits should be based on facts and look as real as possible. Write captions for your displays.

SPACE MYSTERIES

Write an Einstein Anderson mystery using scientific facts about your topic. See if your classmates can solve it.

READ ALL ABOUT IT

Write an article for your school newspaper about your topic. Make it interesting for students who don't know as much about astronomy as you do.

Solar System Maps

Could you find your way from Mars to Jupiter? Make yourself a Solar System map, but plan carefully. If you make it to scale, you'll need a lot of space!

 You Will Need

☐ books on the Solar System, with and without illustrations
☐ mapmaking materials, including poster board, construction paper, glue, and markers or Styrofoam balls

 Procedure

1. There are several ways you can make a map of the Solar System. Decide if you want one that:

- represents the locations and order of the Sun, planets, asteroid belt, and Oort cloud,
- accurately compares the sizes of the Sun and planets,
- represents the distances from planet to planet to scale, or is accurate in size *and* distances.

2. Look through several Solar System books to see the relative sizes of the planets and Sun. Design a 2-D or 3-D map that shows the order and orbits of the planets and asteroid belt around the Sun. You might want to add a comet and the Oort cloud.

3. If you want a mathematical challenge, use the following mathematical formulas to keep your map to scale. You may need the help of an older student.

Use this formula to determine planet sizes:

$$\frac{\text{map diameter of the Sun}}{\text{true diameter of the Sun}} = \frac{\text{map diameter of the planet}}{\text{true diameter of the planet}}$$

Use this formula to determine planet distances:

$$\frac{\text{map diameter of the Sun}}{\text{true diameter of the Sun}} = \frac{\text{map distance from Sun to planet}}{\text{true distance from Sun to planet}}$$

Note: The diameter of the Sun is 865,000 miles. Use the chart on pages 34–35 for diameters of the planets and their average distances from the Sun.

 Digging Deeper

If you tried to make your map to scale, you now know how tough it is to contain the Solar System in your room, school, or even school yard. You might be able to imagine this "Solar System salad" on your way to school or when you take a nature walk with your family. (Your distances will be approximate.)

Start with a pumpkin one foot in diameter to represent the Sun; then add the planets at the suggested distances.

FOR PLANET	USE	DISTANCE FROM PUMPKIN SUN
Mercury	tomato seed	50 feet
Venus	pea	75 feet
Earth	pea	100 feet
Mars	popcorn kernel	175 feet
Jupiter	orange	550 feet
Saturn	peach	1,025 feet
Uranus	plum	2,050 feet
Neptune	tangerine	3,225 feet
Pluto	strawberry seed	1 mile

(NASA quotes this recipe from June 9, 1991, *Parade* magazine.)

One class traced a forty-five-foot Sun on their playground, then calculated distances to, and sizes of, the planets. When they took their class field trip to the science museum, they checked the miles it took to reach the imaginary planets orbiting their school-yard Sun. They were surprised to discover Neptune and Pluto were across the state line!

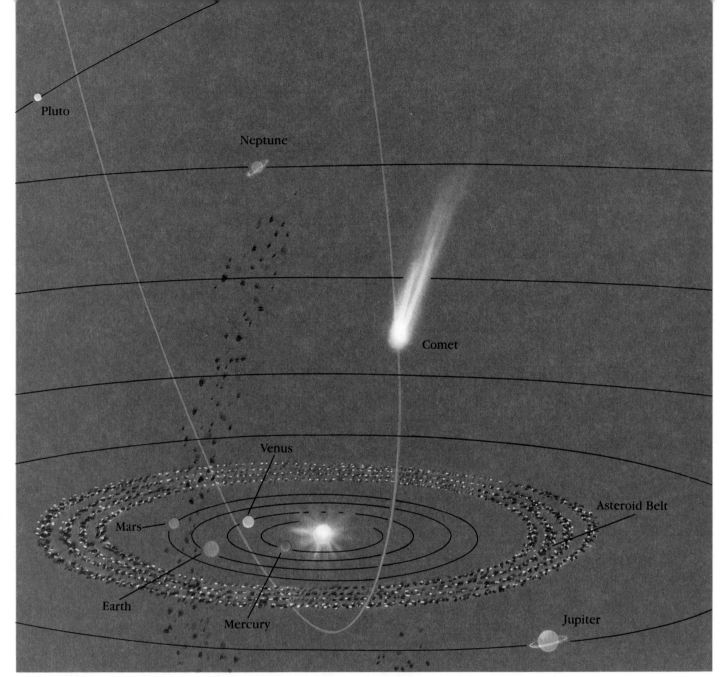

Pluto

Neptune

Comet

Venus

Asteroid Belt

Mars

Earth

Mercury

Jupiter

Saturn's and Uranus's orbits carry them beyond the edges of this map.

IN YOUR JOURNAL

Which better helps you picture the immense size of the Solar System—actually making a map, or reading analogies such as those in the quotation by Seymour Simon (right). Why?

READ MORE ABOUT IT

There are many analogies that make the sizes of the planets more understandable. Go through several astronomy books and see how many you can find.

SEYMOUR SAYS

When I was young, I loved to think about space and how incredibly big things are. But you read a big number in a book and the number just doesn't mean anything. I mean, just how big is the Sun?

If you had a basketball in your hand and used it to represent the Earth, on that scale the Sun would be approximately the size of your school cafeteria or a basketball court. If you put the Earth inside the Sun, like pennies in a piggy bank, you could put one million, three hundred thousand planet Earths in the Sun.

Fantasy Adventures

It will be many years before humans travel to other planets. In the meantime, we can have fun planning.

 YOU WILL NEED

☐ travel brochures (for planet Earth)
☐ books about the planets
☐ sturdy paper
☐ markers, paints, or crayons

 PROCEDURE

1. Look through a number of travel brochures (you can get these at a local travel agency). Which ones make you want to drop everything and go? Why?

2. In small groups, choose several brochures to analyze more closely. Complete two of the activities below:

- Make a list of the facts you think the writer needed to know before writing the brochure. Beside each fact, speculate as to how the information was gathered.
- What words did the writer use to "sell" the location? Make a list of the adjectives and descriptive phrases used.
- The writer needed to get a lot of information into a small space. How did she arrange her words? Did she use complete sentences? How often did she let pictures sell the destination?
- What would make you pick up *this* brochure if it were displayed with fifty others? What catches your eye? How do you think the designer chose the words to set in bold type?

3. Now design your own travel brochure for the planet of your choice. Look through several books on your planet and prepare a brochure that will sell it as a great place to visit.

As you work, ask yourself:

About the planet:

- What are the most interesting locations on the planet?
- Can I plan side trips to moons or rings?
- Are there dangers such as volcanoes, storms, or extreme temperatures? How will tourists be protected?
- How will people travel to the planet? How long will it take to get there?

About the brochure:

- What adjectives and phrases will make the planet sound more inviting?
- How many and what types of pictures should I use?
- How will I design the lettering?

 DIGGING DEEPER

- Set up a Solar System travel agency in your class. Make a display of brochures for others to browse through. Assign agents to help set up trips. Design tickets and travel packages.
- Travelogues are presentations where a guide entertains and educates an audience with pictures and stories of interesting places they've visited. Take a travelogue series on the road to the other classes in your school. Have plenty of descriptions of:

  ○ how you traveled
  ○ the dangers you met along the way
  ○ protective clothing you wore and why you wore it
  ○ sites you visited—moons, craters, rings
  ○ why you want (or don't want) to go back

Images from space probes like Voyager can help us imagine what it would be like to visit Jupiter.

IN YOUR JOURNAL

Use the details from a classmate's brochure to take a fantasy trip. Write a letter home that describes your trip, or design a postcard of your favorite site.

READ MORE ABOUT IT

Fantasy journeys through space are sometimes written realistically; see, for instance, *The NOVA Space Explorer's Guide: Where to Go and What to See*, by Richard Maurer (Crown, 1985). Sometimes authors add humorous or magical elements

to the descriptions; see Joanna Cole's *The Magic School Bus Lost in the Solar System* (Scholastic, 1989). These books may give you some ideas for your own travelogue.

SEYMOUR SAYS

I was once asked if I'd ever gone to Mars. Do I look like I went to Mars? No one on Earth (that we know of) has gone to Mars. I always wanted to go to Mars, but I never had the chance. If any of you have connections about that, please let me know. Maybe we can take a trip together.

Atmospheric Models—
Earth and Venus

Will Earth's atmosphere ever create the kind of greenhouse found on Venus?

 YOU WILL NEED

- ☐ 6 clear jars (or large zip-lock bags)
- ☐ colored sand (you can purchase colored sand or mix powdered tempera with white sand)
  - ☐ 1 jar labeled Earth's Atmosphere
  - ☐ 1 jar labeled Venus's Atmosphere
  - ☐ 1 jar red sand labeled Nitrogen
  - ☐ 1 jar green sand labeled Oxygen
  - ☐ 1 jar blue sand labeled Carbon Dioxide
  - ☐ 1 jar yellow sand labeled Other Gases
- ☐ measuring spoons
- ☐ measuring cups
- ☐ books to explain carbon dioxide and the greenhouse effect

 PROCEDURE

> Percentages of gases in Earth's atmosphere
> 78% nitrogen
> 21% oxygen
> 1% carbon dioxide and trace elements
>
> Percentages of gases in Venus's atmosphere
> 98% carbon dioxide
> 2% other gases

1. Make a sand model of Earth's atmosphere, using different colors of sand to represent the different gases. To help you measure more quickly, note that 16 tablespoons equals 1 cup. For example, 78 tablespoons equals 4 cups plus 14 tablespoons.

- 78 tablespoons of red sand (representing nitrogen)
- 21 tablespoons of green sand (representing oxygen)
- 1 tablespoon of blue sand (representing carbon dioxide)

2. Make a model of Venus's atmosphere by filling the other jar with the following mixture of sand.

- 98 tablespoons of blue sand (representing carbon dioxide)
- 2 tablespoons of yellow sand (representing other gases)

3. Cover and shake each jar.

 DIGGING DEEPER

Look at the amount of carbon dioxide in your model of Earth's atmosphere. Does it take a large percentage of carbon dioxide to keep our planet's surface warm?

In *Venus*, Seymour Simon writes that "Venus's thick atmosphere of carbon dioxide is responsible for the intense heat" on that planet. Compare the amount of carbon dioxide you see in your model of Venus's atmosphere with the amount visible in Earth's. How does the amount of carbon dioxide in the atmosphere affect Earth's temperature? You may need to check more books to help you.

 IN YOUR JOURNAL

Did you know that without greenhouse warming, Earth would be so cold the oceans would freeze? Lucky for us, the carbon dioxide and small traces of other greenhouse gases in our atmosphere trap just enough heat energy to keep the Earth warm.

Write a reassuring letter to a friend in another class who thinks greenhouse warming is always harmful, or write a letter to an adult explaining why we must limit the amount of carbon dioxide released into our atmosphere.

Venus is sometimes called Earth's sister planet because they are about the same size.

 ### READ MORE ABOUT IT

Authors find many different ways (fractions, decimals, graphs) to describe the amount of carbon dioxide in our atmosphere. Look through several encyclopedias or other books to see how many ways you can find. Which seems most precise? Which best helps you visualize the amount of carbon dioxide and other gases?

Mini Greenhouse Planets

Earth and Venus are called sister planets, but Earth's temperatures are nothing like those found on the surface of Venus. By designing your own twin planets and experimenting with the "greenhouses" around them, you can uncover some clues to explain these temperature differences.

 YOU WILL NEED

- ☐ books that describe Venus's greenhouse effect
- ☐ cardboard or heavy paper
- ☐ colored markers
- ☐ scissors
- ☐ a glass or clear plastic jar
- ☐ 2 thermometers

 PROCEDURE

1. Before you begin, think about how it feels when you sit in a car on a sunny day. Now read the explanations of Venus's greenhouse effect in books such as *Venus* and *Our Solar System*.

2. Trace, color, and cut out two identical circles, small enough to fit inside the jar. Make sure they are colored exactly the same so that they will absorb and reflect the same amount of heat.

3. Place planet 1 on a sunny windowsill or table. Lay a thermometer across the "planet."

4. Place planet 2 in a jar with the other thermometer. Seal the jar tightly and set it next to planet 1 in the sunlight. *Make sure both planets are receiving the same amount of light.*

5. Check and record the temperatures of both planets after five minutes. Repeat every five minutes for half an hour. Which planet is hotter?

6. Check the thermometers again every five minutes after the planets are no longer in direct sunlight. What do you notice about the temperatures?

7. Keep track of your planets' temperatures on a graph. At the end of the period, write one or two sentences analyzing your data.

 DIGGING DEEPER

- Use your graph to compare the temperatures of planets 1 and 2. When were the temperatures most similar? When were they the most different?
- In *Venus,* the author explains why the inside of a car gets so hot in the sun. How does this help explain what happened to your mini planets?

 IN YOUR JOURNAL

Brainstorm a list of factors that could change planet 2's temperature (such as leaving off the lid or covering the planet with cotton). Then choose one factor from your list and predict its effect. Design an experiment to test your prediction.

 READ MORE ABOUT IT

In many science-fiction stories, people live in protected environments and always wear space suits when they venture outside. Compare the setting in several science-fiction stories, focusing on the atmospheres the authors describe.

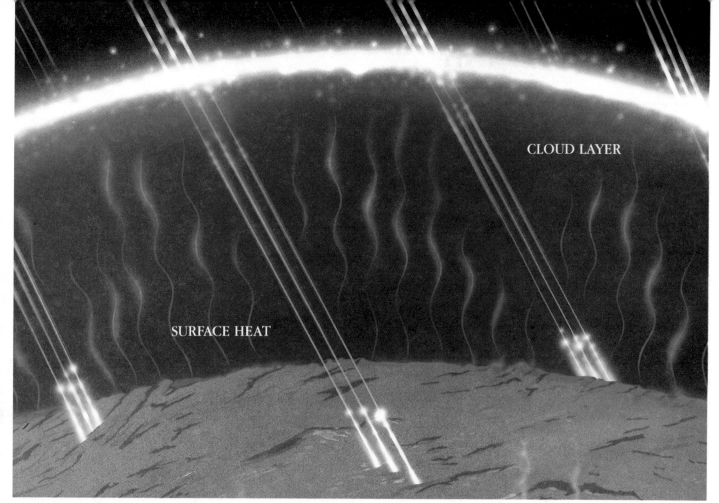

Sunlight passes through Venus's atmosphere of carbon dioxide and heats the rocky surface. The rocks radiate heat and the atmosphere traps the heat, creating a greenhouse effect.

MINI GREENHOUSE PLANET TEMPERATURE DATA

TIME	LIGHT CONDITIONS	TEMPERATURE PLANET 1	TEMPERATURE PLANET 2

Oceans of Air

Riddle: When can you see the Sun after it has set?
Answer: Any clear evening, because just when the Sun appears to be setting, it is actually below the horizon!
    This activity will help explain why.

 YOU WILL NEED

☐ a partner to work with
☐ a pencil
☐ a clear glass half filled with water
☐ a coin
☐ an empty mug
☐ water

 PROCEDURE

1. Place the pencil in the glass of water (eraser end out of the water) and bend your head to the level of the glass. Discuss with your partner how and why you think the pencil's appearance has changed. Set the glass aside.

2. Place the coin in the bottom of the empty mug. Partner 1: Place your head so that the coin is totally blocked by the edge of the mug—but is *just* out of sight.

3. Partner 2: Slowly pour water into the mug, making sure you don't disturb the position of the coin.

4. Partner 1: Keep your head and eyes steady. What do you see when your classmate pours water into the mug?

 DIGGING DEEPER

• Light travels faster through air than through water. This causes light to bend when passing from one medium to another. What ideas do you have about why the pencil looked broken

or why the coin suddenly appeared at the bottom of the mug?

• How do you think the water vapor in our atmosphere affects our view of stars and planets? Why would viewing something through water *vapor* be different from viewing it through a solid body of water?

• Seymour Simon suggests (in *Our Solar System*) that our planet could be named Oceans or Water, because it is the only planet with large amounts of liquid water on its surface and vapor in its atmosphere. How do you think all this water affects how our planet looks *from* space?

 IN YOUR JOURNAL

Draw a diagram or write several sentences to explain the riddle at the beginning of this chapter. Use the coin and mug activity to help you.

 READ MORE ABOUT IT

Water has many unique and remarkable properties. Using both experiment books and descriptions of water, see how many properties you can list.

 SEYMOUR SAYS

I became an author while I was a teacher. I wanted to use a lot of books in class, but often I couldn't find any. For example, we used to make paper airplanes in class, and I couldn't find a book that showed how to make paper airplanes

in a simple way. So I decided that I would write one.

My editor's office was on the sixteenth floor in a New York City high rise. One day, to test the airplanes from my book, we stood at her window and sailed the airplanes we'd just folded.

You can just imagine the looks on the faces of the people in the building across the street.

Creating Blue Skies

Take a look at planet Earth. Is it any wonder it's often called the blue planet? Beaming a light through some soapy water can help demonstrate why our skies appear so blue—from above and below.

 YOU WILL NEED

☐ 2 clear glasses or plastic cups
☐ water
☐ soap
☐ a flashlight
☐ foil
☐ a nail
☐ a prism

 PROCEDURE

1. Fill two glasses with water. Dissolve a sliver of soap into the water in one glass, then wait for the water to become clear again.

2. Wrap the end of the flashlight in foil and use the nail to poke a small hole in the center of the foil.

3. While you are waiting for the soapy water to clear, take a look at the clear white light of sunshine coming through a sunny window. (Do not look directly at the Sun.)

4. Hold a prism up to the light of the Sun. Turn it until you see the light separated into its rainbow of colors—red, orange, yellow, green, blue, and violet. Light waves come in many lengths. The longest waves are red light, and the shortest waves are blue and violet. As light passes through the prism, it is bent and spreads out into its rainbow, or spectrum, of colors.

5. When your soapy water appears fairly clear, darken the room. Holding the flashlight to the side of the glass, pass the light horizontally through the nonsoapy water. Then pass the light through the soapy water in exactly the same way. What differences do you see in the color of the two light beams?

6. Look closely at the light passing through the soapy water. What differences do you see in the color of the light entering and exiting the glass?

What is happening? As light passes through the water, it hits and bounces off the tiny soapy particles. Like light bending through a prism, it is then broken into a spectrum of colors. The colors with the shortest wavelengths—the blue and violet—scatter, so they are visible to our eyes. The longer wavelengths of light (yellow, orange, and red) continue on through the water.

 DIGGING DEEPER

Light passing through the soapy water is similar to the light that reaches Earth. Sunlight passes through an atmosphere filled with water vapor and dust. As sunlight hits the tiny particles, it is broken into its rainbow of colors. The blue light scatters from molecule to molecule, surrounding the Earth in a blanket of blue. This is called Rayleigh scattering.

- Light travels the longest distance to our eyes when the Sun sits on the horizon. How do the colors exiting the soapy water illustrate what we see at sunrise and sunset?
- See if you can find a pair of blue-blocker sunglasses. (These are often used by people taking part in outdoor sports.) How does their use change how you see the colors of things?

 IN YOUR JOURNAL

Look at photos of Mercury and our Moon, places with very little atmosphere. Write or draw a description of how you think Earth would appear from space if it were not surrounded by its atmosphere.

A photograph of Earth taken by the Apollo 15 astronauts on their way home from the Moon.

 READ MORE ABOUT IT

Locate several picture books that contain illustrations of the sky. Seymour Simon's *Weather* (Morrow, 1993) and *Storms* (Morrow, 1989) contain dramatic photographs. Tomie de Paola's *The Cloud Book* (Holiday House, 1975) uses cartoon-like illustrations, and *Mojave*, by Diane Siebert (Harper & Row, 1988), is based upon a glorious series of paintings by Wendell Minor. Try describing the sky on a page from each of the books and see if a friend can use your description to find the illustration you had in mind.

Planetary Birthdays

How many candles would be on your birthday cake if you'd lived your whole life on Mercury, Mars, or Pluto?

 YOU WILL NEED

☐ a calculator (or pencil and paper)

 PROCEDURE

Mercury, Venus, and Mars

Because these planets don't take very long to travel around the Sun, it will be easiest to do these calculations in *days*.

1. First, determine how many days old you are. One way to do this is to multiply your age by 365 and then add the number of days that have passed since your last birthday.

Formula: _____ × 365 + _____ = age in days
(years old)   *(days since birthday)*

Example: *If it is forty-six days past your tenth birthday, you will multiply 10 times 365 days in a year and add 46.*

$$(10 \times 365) + 46 = \text{days old}$$
$$3{,}650 \quad + 46 = \text{days old}$$
$$3{,}696 \text{ days old}$$

2. Use the chart below to determine how many Earth days are in one year on your planet. For example, one Mercury year is eighty-eight days.

3. Divide the number of days in the planet's year into the number of days you are old.

Formula:
$$\frac{\text{days old}}{\text{days in planet's year}}$$

PLANETS OF THE SOLAR SYSTEM

	MERCURY	**VENUS**	**EARTH**	**MARS**
Average distance from Sun in miles and kilometers	36 million miles/ 58 million km	67 million miles/ 108 million km	93 million miles/ 150 million km	141 million miles/ 228 million km
Revolution in Earth days, Earth years	88 days	224.7 days	365.26 days	687 days
Rotation in Earth days, hours, minutes	58.6 days	243 days	23 hours, 56 min, 4 sec	24 hours, 37 min, 23 sec
Equatorial diameter in miles	3,031	7,519	7,926.6	4,221
Atmosphere; main gases	almost none	carbon dioxide	nitrogen, oxygen	carbon dioxide
Surface gravity (Earth = 1)	0.38	0.91	1	0.38
Number of known satellites	0	0	1	2
Rings	0	0	0	0

Example: *If you are 3,696 days old, divide 3,696 by 88 to determine how many Mercury years you've been around.*

$$\frac{3,696}{88} = 42$$ You would be forty-two years old on Mercury.

4. You may have noticed that this formula does not take leap years into account. If you wish, add those extra days (one every four years) to your space age.

Jupiter, Saturn, Uranus, Neptune, and Pluto

It takes so long for these planets to travel around the Sun, their revolutions are given in Earth *years*. You may wish to round off your age to the closest year when figuring out how old you'd be on these outer planets.

1. To determine your age on a planet *beyond* Mars, simply divide your age by the Earth years it takes for that planet to revolve around the Sun.

Formula: $$\frac{\text{your age in years}}{\text{planet's revolution in Earth years}}$$

Example: *If you are twelve years old and want to know your Uranus age, divide 12 by 84.*

$$\frac{12}{84} = \frac{1}{7}$$ or 0.1428571 years (about 52 Earth days)

 ### In Your Journal

Use the comparisons of the planets' rotations in Earth days, hours, and minutes to determine on which planet your actual birth *day* would last the longest. Where in the Solar System would you like to hold your birthday party. Why?

 ### Read More about It

Look at several books that explain the rotations and revolutions of the planets. What makes one explanation more appealing than another? Which is easiest to understand? Why?

JUPITER	SATURN	URANUS	NEPTUNE	PLUTO
483.4 million miles/ 778.3 million km	886.7 million miles/ 1,427 million km	1,783 million miles/ 2,870 million km	2,794 million miles/ 4,497 million km	3,666 million miles/ 5,900 million km
11.86 years	29.46 years	84 years	164.8 years	248 years
9 hours, 55 min	10 hours, 40 min	17 hours, 14 min	18 hours, 30 min (?)	6 days, 9 hours
88,734	74,977	32,000	30,540	1,430 (approximate)
hydrogen, helium	hydrogen, helium	helium, hydrogen, methane	hydrogen, helium, methane	very thin methane (?)
2.64	1.13	1.17	1.19	.08 (?)
16	21	15	8	1
1	1,000 (?)	11 (?)	4	0

Planetary Storms

Can you imagine a single hurricane that lasted for centuries? In this activity, you will learn more about a giant storm on Jupiter that has not changed its position for hundreds of years.

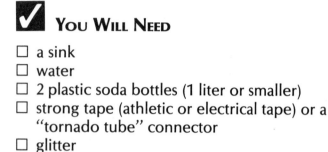 **YOU WILL NEED**

- ☐ a sink
- ☐ water
- ☐ 2 plastic soda bottles (1 liter or smaller)
- ☐ strong tape (athletic or electrical tape) or a "tornado tube" connector
- ☐ glitter
- ☐ books on Jupiter

PROCEDURE

1. Jupiter's storm is similar to a hurricane on Earth. Both are types of vortexes—whirlpools of liquid spinning around an area of relative calm, which is called the eye. Maybe you've observed this phenomenon as the water drains from your bath.

Try reproducing the movement of Jupiter's giant storm in a sink in your kitchen or class. Fill your sink about halfway. Swirl your hand around, making a circular motion in the water. Then remove the stopper and watch the movement of the water swirling into the cavity of your drain.

2. You can view a vortex from a different angle by connecting two clear bottles with strong tape (you can also use a "tornado tube," available in science and toy stores, but making your own will get you the same results). Fill one bottle with water, about one-third full. Add some glitter to the water to see how more solid matter moves in a vortex.

3. Place the opening of the empty bottle directly on top of the bottle with the water.

4. Tightly wrap a piece of tape around the two bottle necks.

5. Hold the bottles securely at the point where they connect.

6. Quickly invert the bottles so that the one with the water is on top. As soon as they are flipped, rapidly rotate the bottles in a circular motion. (Pretend you are tracing an imaginary circle with the upturned end of the bottle—it might feel like twirling a lasso.)

7. Once the water is spinning, rest the bottles on a tabletop and watch the motion of the water from all sides. Where is the eye of this storm-in-a-bottle?

 DIGGING DEEPER

- Use your books to read about Jupiter and its Great Red Spot. Compare what you learned in your books with the information your classmates got from their reading.
- Look at the photos of the giant storm. Compare and contrast them with pictures of storms in Earth's atmosphere such as the typhoon over the Pacific in *Our Solar System*.
- Through your reading and activity, can you develop any theories about Jupiter's Great Red Spot? Astronomers are still working on theirs.

 IN YOUR JOURNAL

Locate two pictures of Jupiter taken at different times. (Two photos, taken four months apart, are

The Great Red Spot, a giant storm on Jupiter nearly three times the size of Earth.

on one page in *Jupiter*.) Compare the appearance of Jupiter's storm with the rest of the clouds on the planet.

Draw a line down the center of a page in your journal. On one side make a list of your observations. On the other side make a list of questions.

 READ MORE ABOUT IT

Experiment books often describe activities like the one presented here. Look through several of these books. What makes for easy-to-follow and inviting instructions?

Robot Explorers

Human travel to other planets appears unlikely at this time, but with the help of special spacecraft many scientists are already exploring the mysteries of our Solar System neighbors. In this activity, you'll have a chance to design your own robot explorer to send to distant worlds.

 ### SEYMOUR SAYS

In the time it takes for a ball to drop from my hand to the floor, a spaceship would travel about ten miles. At that speed, I could go from Washington, D.C., to New York City in about forty seconds, but it still would take a year to get to Mars. If you're going to take that long a trip, you might as well spend a few days.

We don't know if anybody could live on Mars for long. They'd need food, water, oxygen, videotapes, and all the other things people need in order to exist.

So when we sent spaceships to Mars, nobody went. We sent Viking landers and spaceships loaded with instruments but no people.

 ### YOU WILL NEED

- ☐ books about planets
- ☐ books and magazines about robots and planetary exploration
- ☐ pencils, markers, crayons, and paper
- ☐ clay or building sets

 ### PROCEDURE

1. Before you begin, look through several books about the planets. With a partner, discuss what hazards your space explorer would meet on the different planets.

2. Read about the robots that are already being planned and used. Discuss the pros and cons of a few designs. For example, some scientists think "rovers" will work the best. Others believe we should send a swarm of insect robots, like Genghis, a six-legged antlike robot that weighs only two pounds.

3. Choose a planet you would like to know more about, design an exploratory mission to that planet, and draw or construct a robot to send.

4. As you plan your mission, decide whether you want to collect a lot of information from one place or get a sampling of data from a larger area. Are you interested only in the surface, or do you want to learn about the atmosphere?

5. As you design your robot, think about how it will operate. Will it move on wheels or feet? Will it crawl, walk, or hop? Why? How will it receive instructions from Earth, and how will it return the data it has collected? Will you need one robot or an entire fleet?

6. Don't forget to think about the hazards your robot might run into as it moves about the planet. Refer to your books often to study your planet's features: surface, atmosphere, storms, volcanoes, and temperatures.

 ### DIGGING DEEPER

- Collaborate with your classmates by sharing ideas in group conference meetings. Scientists often work together in teams so that they can use the best ideas from everyone. What ideas did your classmates put in their explorers that you could adapt for your model?
- Before an expensive model is sent to a distant planet, it will need to be tested on Earth. As a group, develop a plan for testing the designs of the robot models in your class. You could develop a checklist or perhaps exchange designs in a peer-review process.

The Viking landers were the first American robot explorers to land on another planet.

 IN YOUR JOURNAL

Draw a line halfway down the middle of a page. On the left, list several features of the planet your robot was designed to explore. On the right, list the similar features of another planet. On the bottom of the page, write or draw some of the changes you would have to make to your robot so that it could be used to explore the second planet.

 READ MORE ABOUT IT

Gloria Skurzynski, in *Robots: Your High-Tech World* (Bradbury, 1990), George Harrar, in *Radical Robots: Can You Be Replaced?* (Simon and Schuster, 1990), and Fredericka Berger, in *Robots: What They Are, What They Do* (Greenwillow, 1992), all describe robots currently in use. Alfred B. Bortz, in *Superstuff!* (Watts, 1990), tells us about materials that have changed our lives. After looking through these books, feel free to improve the design of your robot.

Exploring Venus

How can we "see" the surface of a planet wrapped in layers of thick, dense atmosphere? This was the problem facing astronomers when they tried to study Venus. Read on to see how they solved the problem. Then try an activity that will have you "seeing" a hidden surface.

 YOU WILL NEED

- ☐ books with pictures of Venus
- ☐ a small rubber ball
- ☐ a gift box with lid (about 3 inches high)
- ☐ enough clay to fill the bottom of the box
- ☐ 2 pieces of graph paper
- ☐ scissors
- ☐ rubber cement
- ☐ a nail
- ☐ a long thin stick that will not be needed after this activity (a thin dowel or chopstick)
- ☐ a ruler
- ☐ colored markers

PROCEDURE

1. Locate contour maps made from data collected by the Pioneer Venus Orbiter. One is reproduced in Seymour Simon's *Venus*. On this map, the mountains and valleys of Venus's surface are shown in different colors. Orange and red areas represent taller regions than those shown in blue.

2. NASA used remote sensing to map Venus's hidden surface. A radar device sent out signals and then measured the time it took for the signals to bounce back.

Here's a way you can demonstrate this: Sit three feet from a friend. Roll her the ball and have her roll it back immediately. Repeat this several times, each time sitting farther and farther apart. (Try to roll the ball at the same speed each time.)

- At which distance did it take the longest time for the ball to return?
- At which distance did it take the ball the shortest time to return?

- What could you determine about distance if you knew the speed at which the ball traveled and the length of time its round-trip took?

3. Now you can make your own map of a hidden surface. Fill the bottom of the gift box with clay, making the surface very tall in some places, very shallow in others.

4. Cut a piece of graph paper the size of the box lid. Label the paper with one number in each square down the left side of the paper, and one letter in each square across the top of the paper.

5. Glue the paper on the box lid. Use the nail to poke a hole in each square of the graph paper. Place the lid on the box.

6. Label a second piece of graph paper exactly as you labeled the paper on the box lid. This is your map. (Do not poke holes in this paper.)

7. Make six marks on the stick, one every half inch. Color each half-inch section a different color. This is your probe.

8. You are now ready to begin making your map.

- Locate the hole on your box lid labeled A-1.
- Insert your probe until it touches the surface of the clay.
- To what color on the stick have you inserted your probe?
- On your map, color the square A-1 that color.

9. Move to B-1. Insert the probe until it touches the surface of the clay. What color is the probe inserted to? Color the square B-1 on your map that color.

10. Continue across the first row. Repeat on each row until you have surveyed the entire hidden surface with your probe.

 DIGGING DEEPER

- Which colors on your map represent the tallest peaks on your hidden surface? Which colors

on your map represent the shallowest valleys?
- See if you can use the map made by someone else to reproduce his or her hidden surface.

  IN YOUR JOURNAL and **READ MORE ABOUT IT**

Lots of books are written in diary form. Read *Pedro's Journal*, by Pam Conrad (Caroline House, 1991), or any other diary. In your journal, describe the journey of someone crossing the area you have just mapped.

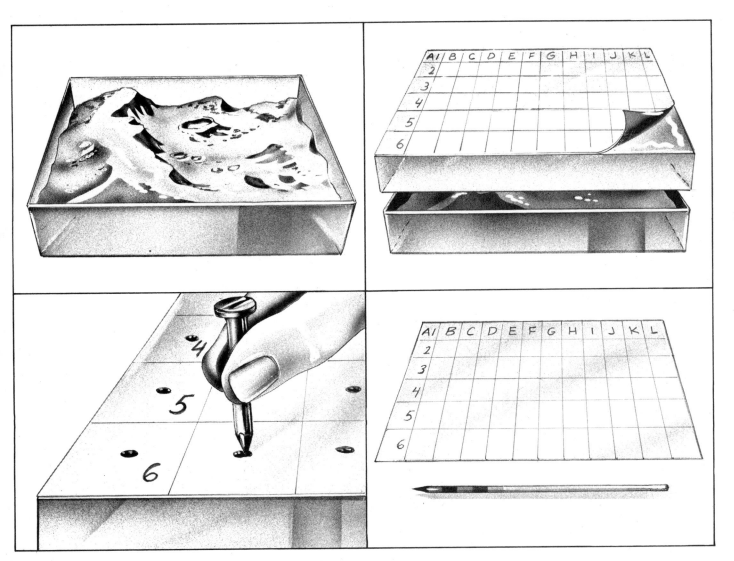

Impact!

Four billion years of meteorites and asteroids crashing into a planet's surface can leave it pretty scarred. But are the craters on each planet the same? Try this activity for a look at some of the factors affecting the cratered surfaces of our Solar System.

 YOU WILL NEED

- ☐ books about planets, meteors, comets, and asteroids
- ☐ shallow baking pans or sturdy box lids
- ☐ materials to make different "planet surfaces," such as wet and dry sand, clay, soil, flour, peppercorns
- ☐ different-sized "meteors," such as marbles, pebbles, or beans
- ☐ plaster of paris
- ☐ water
- ☐ paper
- ☐ towel

PROCEDURE

1. Each planet and moon is unique—each has its own surface and atmosphere. Look at the cratered surfaces pictured at right. Compare these with pictures of other planetary surfaces.

2. Design your own planetary surface by packing a pan with at least two inches of wet or dry sand, clay, or soil, and then bombard it with "meteorites."

- Drop a pebble or marble onto the surface. After impact, gently remove your artificial meteorite and inspect the crater.
- Try different-sized meteorites launched from different angles. What do you notice about the craters?
- Experiment with different materials for your planet surface. Make your planet dusty by

sprinkling flour over the surface. Make it rocky by scattering beans or peppercorns.

3. As you go, diagram your findings, indicating size of meteor, speed (slow, fast, very fast) and angle (overhead, small angle, sharp angle) of impact, and resulting craters.

4. Make a permanent model of your cratered planet to display in your classroom. Here's how:

- Fill a pan with at least two inches of wet plaster of paris.
- Experiment with a variety of meteor sizes and angles of entry.
- On a paper the same size and shape as your planet, chart where and how each impact was made. Display your meteors, chart, and permanent craters together.

5. How does a blanket of atmosphere protect a planet's surface? See if you can design an experiment that will test this question. Here's one way you could use a towel to represent the atmosphere surrounding Venus or Earth.

- Prepare a fresh sandy surface. Cover half of the surface with a layer of towel or other soft material to simulate how the atmosphere cushions the larger meteors and prevents smaller ones from impacting.
- Drop several meteors of different sizes on each side of the surface.
- Remove the towel and compare the craters.

Craters on the Moon (left) and Mercury.

Digging Deeper

- In *Venus,* we read that, due to Venus's atmosphere, there are no craters smaller than about four miles across. Look again at some of your books. What *might* you be able to conclude about a planet's atmosphere simply by looking at the pictures?
- You can read about one close encounter Earth had with a meteor in Seymour Simon's *Comets, Meteors, and Asteroids.* Once again, our atmosphere served as a protective shield against impact. A large collision with Earth did occur about 50,000 years ago. See if you can find pictures of this massive crater, located in Arizona.

In Your Journal and Read More about It

Some scientists think that Earth's collision with an asteroid or large meteor caused the extinction of the dinosaurs. Several books describe theories about how dinosaurs became extinct. See, for instance, Franklyn Branley's *What Happened to the Dinosaurs?* (HarperCollins, 1989) or Seymour Simon's *New Q & A's about Dinosaurs* (Morrow, 1990). What do you think about these theories?

43

Comparing Craters

Take a look at some photos of the cratered planets and their moons. How can astronomers tell the difference between impact and volcanic craters? Read on to see if you can tell the difference.

 YOU WILL NEED

☐ books about the planets
☐ colored sand (you can make your own by mixing powdered tempera paint with white sand)
☐ a shallow baking pan or sturdy box lid
☐ pebbles
☐ cornstarch
☐ water

 PROCEDURE

1. Use your books to compare the differences between impact craters and volcanic craters. You will discover that:

Volcanic craters are formed when a volcano's peak collapses into a hole. Because it collapses *inward,* no rocky debris is scattered outside the crater. However, lava may flow out of the crater to outlying areas and harden there.

Impact craters are caused when meteors crash into a planet's surface. The meteorite usually breaks up on impact and mixes with rocky debris scattered on the planetary surface.

2. If you have *Venus,* by Seymour Simon, find the picture of three large meteorite-impact craters. On the opposite page are seven domed volcanic hills. Using the photos and text, list some of the differences between the two sets of craters.

3. If you have completed **Impact!** (page 42), take a closer look at your craters. Now you will make some new craters, this time looking at how the rim forms and how debris is scattered.

* Spread several layers of colored sand in a shallow pan. List the order of sand colors from deepest to shallowest.
* Drop a pebble onto the sandy surface. Before you remove it, examine the sur- roundings closely. Carefully remove the pebble and examine the crater it left behind. What did the impact do to the surface layers?

4. Like meteor impacts, volcanoes change the look of the surface surrounding them. Often, lava spills over the edge and fills nearby cracks and craters. See if you can find photos where this has happened. In *Venus,* you will see the Golubkina crater. It looks like an impact crater flooded by lava that hardened flat and smooth.

5. Lava is melted rock that pours out of erupting volcanoes. It molds to the shape of the surrounding surface, then hardens. You can see how difficult it is to contain a substance like lava by mixing some water and cornstarch.

* Mix cornstarch and water into a thick, wet consistency.
* Take one or two spoonfuls into your hands and pack the material tightly into a ball.
* Open your hand and pass the ball to your neighbor. How long does it keep its shape?

 DIGGING DEEPER

* Use photos in your books to compare pictures of several volcanoes. You might look for the largest known volcano, Olympus Mons, located near the Martian equator. Or look for Jupiter's moon Io, the only moon in the Solar System with active volcanoes. How might its volcanoes' flows of liquid sulfur change the moon's surface?
* With a partner, list all the facts you can find about the surface of one planet or moon. Then compare your list with those of your class- mates. Which features are common and which are unique among the planets and moons?

The surface of Mercury is heavily cratered.

IN YOUR JOURNAL

What do you think we can and cannot learn about volcanoes on other planets by studying volcanoes on Earth?

READ MORE ABOUT IT

Seymour Simon and Patricia Lauber are two people who have written books about volcanoes *and* space. How would studying Earth science

help you understand and write about space topics?

SEYMOUR SAYS

I've always been the kind of person who loves to tell people about what I've learned. When I was a kid, people would ask me questions, and I always told them more than they wanted to know. That's what inspired me to write about all kinds of science in my books.

Giant Magnets

You are probably familiar with small magnets that can fit in the palm of your hand, but did you ever think of a planet as a giant magnet? Read on to see how you can make a model of the Earth and its magnetic field.

 ## You Will Need

- ☐ books that illustrate magnetic fields surrounding the planets
- ☐ a thin dowel
- ☐ a Styrofoam ball, about 2 to 3 inches in diameter
- ☐ permanent markers in two colors
- ☐ several pipe cleaners, about 12 inches long

 ## Procedure

1. Look through several books for illustrations describing the magnetic fields around the planets. The diagram on page 49 is from Seymour Simon's *Uranus*. The planet's magnetic field is illustrated by the blue lines. The magnetic poles are where the arcs come together at the planet's surface.

In this picture, the poles labeled *N* and *S* are the geographic poles. They mark the axis on which the planet rotates. (You can picture a planet's axis as an imaginary giant stick poked through its center. The planet spins around this axis.)

Uranus is unusual because its geographic and magnetic poles are very far apart. Unlike Uranus, Earth's magnetic poles are very close to its geographic poles.

2. To make your Earth model, poke a dowel directly through the center of a Styrofoam ball. Color code the ends of the dowel to mark the north and south poles.

3. Because Earth's magnetic pole is so close to its axis, you can mark its magnetic north and south poles at those same locations. (On a larger model you would need to show they are not exactly the same.)

4. Poke one end of a pipe cleaner into magnetic north. Bend the pipe cleaner around the ball and poke the other end into the magnetic south pole. Repeat with several pipe cleaners to illustrate the three-dimensional magnetic field that surrounds the Earth. This magnetic field is called the magnetosphere.

5. Use illustrations from books to make models of the magnetospheres surrounding other planets.

 ## Digging Deeper

- Electrically charged particles from the Sun are trapped at the poles of Earth's giant magnetic field and create spectacular light shows in the sky. These are called the aurora borealis, or northern lights, at the north pole, and the aurora australis, or southern lights, at the south pole. See if you can find pictures of these to share with your classmates.
- Find out which planets do not produce strong magnetic fields.

 ## In Your Journal

Use your model Earth to draw the magnetosphere from different angles. What does it look like when viewed from above the poles? What would it look like if you sliced through the center of the Earth and its magnetosphere?

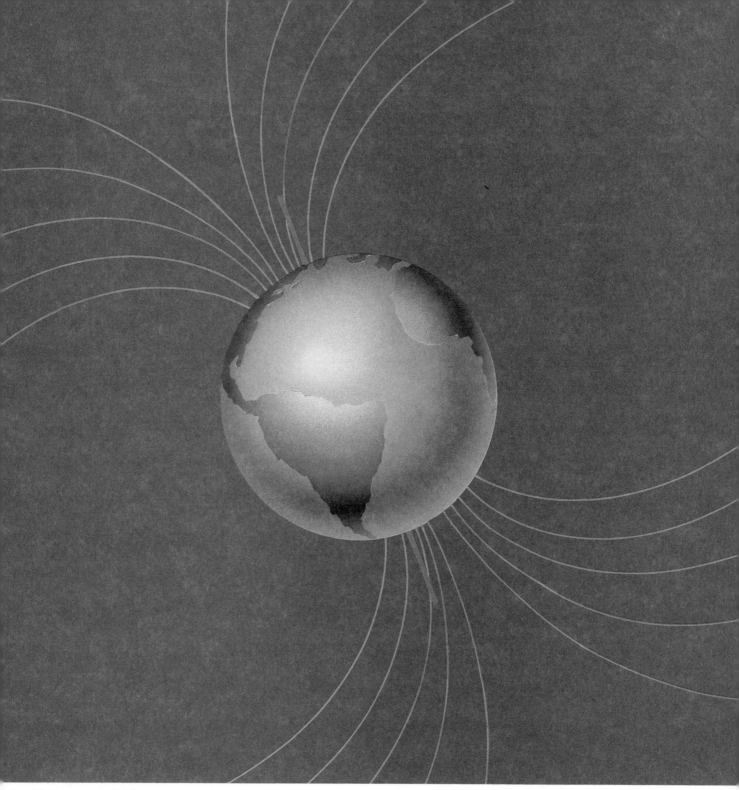

Earth's magnetic field.

 ## READ MORE ABOUT IT

Take a look at a book like *The Way Things Work,* by David Macaulay (Houghton Mifflin, 1988); *How Everyday Things Work,* by Chris Cooper and Tony Osmond (Orbis, 1984); or *The Macmillan Book of How Things Work,* by Michael and Marcia Folsom (Macmillan, 1987). Do any of the workings use magnets? How might you improve an invention by adding a magnet? For more information on improving inventions see *Mistakes That Worked,* by Charlotte Foltz Jones (Doubleday, 1991), or *Inventions and Discoveries,* by Geoff Endacott (Viking, 1991).

Finding Magnetic North

Have you ever used a compass to find north? Here's an activity with magnets and a compass to explore how a compass works.

 YOU WILL NEED

- ☐ a bar magnet
- ☐ very thin string, such as one strand of embroidery floss
- ☐ tape or rulers
- ☐ a compass

 PROCEDURE

1. See for yourself how even a small magnet is affected by Earth's giant magnetic field. Tie one end of the string to the north pole of the bar magnet, the other end to the south pole.

2. Attach the center of the string to the bottom of a shelf, the top of a doorway, or anywhere that the bar magnet is suspended in the air and can rotate freely. When the magnet stops turning, note the direction in which it points.

3. Tap the magnet gently to start it turning again. When it stops, note the direction in which it rests. Place a marker on the floor (a strip of tape or a ruler), showing the direction in which the magnet came to rest.

4. Repeat in several locations in your room. What do you notice about the directions of your markers?

5. Remove the magnet. Lay a compass on the markers on the floor. In what direction does the compass needle point?

 DIGGING DEEPER

- When left to swing freely, the bar magnet will always come to rest along Earth's magnetic lines of force. With a partner, test the directions of swinging bar magnets in several locations in your school and homes.
- In step 5, why was it important to remove the magnet before using the compass? How would its magnetic field have affected the compass needle?
- Look at the model you made in the **Giant Magnets** activity, or find pictures of Earth's geographic and magnetic poles. How does a compass help you locate the north pole on the Earth?

 IN YOUR JOURNAL

In this diagram of Uranus, you can see how its magnetosphere is not in line with its axis. If you were in a spaceship traveling around the planet Uranus, would a magnetic compass help you find Uranus's geographic north pole? Why or why not?

 READ MORE ABOUT IT

You can read another version of this activity in *How to Be a Space Scientist in Your Own Home,* by Seymour Simon (Lippincott, 1982). Do any of the other activities Mr. Simon describes intrigue you?

Solar Wind

N

S

Magnetosphere

Uranus's magnetic field.

Storms on the Sun

Planets are not the only objects in the Solar System with magnetic fields. You can read about powerful magnetic storms on our closest star in books like The Sun, *and in activities like this one you can see firsthand evidence of these storms.*

> **CAUTION:** NEVER LOOK DIRECTLY AT THE SUN—WITH OR WITHOUT BINOCULARS. LOOKING AT THE SUN CAN BLIND YOU.

 YOU WILL NEED

- ☐ a sunny day
- ☐ stiff white paper or poster board
- ☐ binoculars—you may want to cover one eyepiece so that you do not get two images of the Sun
- ☐ books about the Sun

 PROCEDURE

1. Prop a piece of poster board so that it is directly in the Sun's light.

2. Hold or prop the binoculars about two feet away, so that they are pointed toward the Sun. The eyepieces should be pointed at the paper.

> REMEMBER, YOU SHOULD NOT LOOK THROUGH THE BINOCULARS AT THE SUN.

3. Adjust the position of the binoculars until you get the Sun's bright image on the paper. You may also need to adjust the focus.

4. Any dark dots you see on the Sun's image are sunspots.

You can track the rotation of the sunspots by repeating this activity on several sunny days.

1. Set up the binoculars and poster board as you did in steps 1 through 3.

2. Trace an outline of the Sun's image on the poster board. (You may need a classmate to hold the binoculars steady while you draw.)

3. Mark the date and location of each sunspot.

4. Repeat this procedure each sunny day, adjusting your setup so that the Sun's image falls exactly inside the circle you drew on day one.

 DIGGING DEEPER

- Imagine how large the magnetic storms on the Sun must be to show up on your poster board 93,000,000 miles away. Look in books like *The Sun* for details of their sizes. Make a list of words and phrases that describe the powerful forces that produce these sunspots.
- What can you find out about the magnetic forces on the Sun? How are they similar to magnetic forces on planets? How are they different?

 IN YOUR JOURNAL

Galileo used the movement of sunspots across the surface of the Sun to prove that the Sun rotates. Pretend you are Galileo and explain to a ten-year-old child how these moving spots could prove the Sun's rotation.

 READ MORE ABOUT IT

Because the Sun is visible during our waking hours, it is an easy target for study. Try some of the activities from the excellent *Anno's Sundial,* by Mitsumasa Anno (Philomel, 1987), or the older but still available *Catch a Sunbeam: A Book of Solar Study and Experiments,* by Florence Adams (Harcourt Brace, 1978).

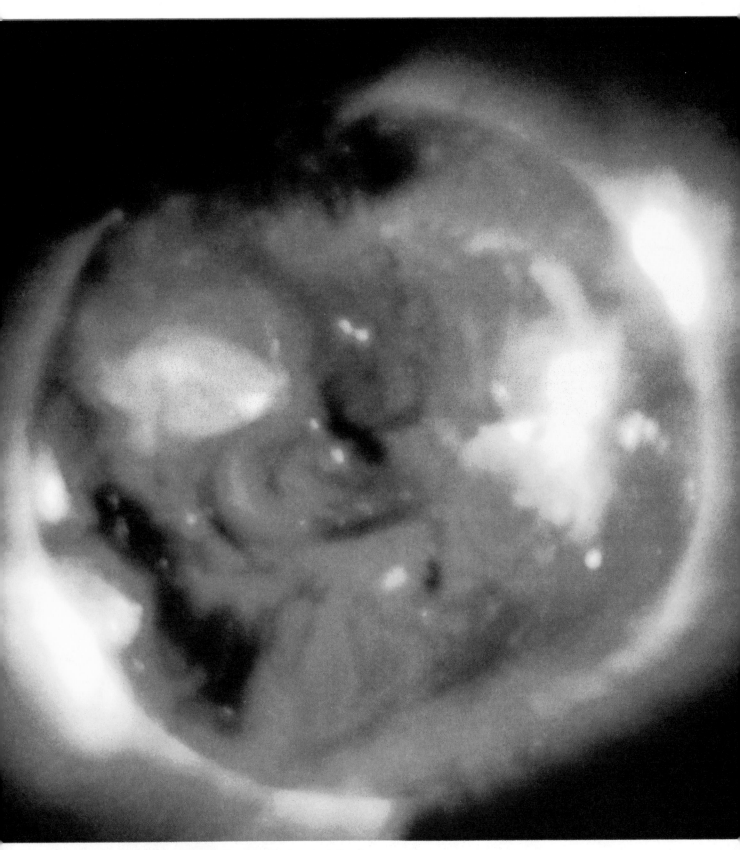

Magnetic forces are released in violent explosions on the Sun.

Space Olympics

How much weight could you lift in a competition on Mars? Could you throw the javelin farther on Venus or on Saturn? What type of obstacle course could you make on Mercury?

 ## You Will Need

- [ ] Seymour Simon's *Einstein Anderson Lights Up the Sky* (Viking Press, 1982)
- [ ] information on the surface gravity of the nine planets (Use the chart on this page or, for more accurate results, use the chart on pages 34–35.)
- [ ] a chart to convert your Earth scores to planet scores (Use the chart on this page or devise one of your own.)

 ## Procedure

1. Read the condensed version of "The Lunar Olympics," on page 90, or the complete story in *Einstein Anderson Lights Up the Sky*. Then use the ideas from the story and the discussion questions on this page to help your class set up a fantasy Olympics for our Solar System.

2. Divide the class into eight groups—one for each planet other than Earth.

3. In your group, design one Olympic contest for your planet. Remember, your event doesn't need to be the same as any of those held on Earth, but it should take advantage of the gravity and physical features of your planet.

4. List and collect the materials you will need so that visiting athletes can actually compete in your contest. Do you need scales? Weights?

5. Decide how you will convert Earth scores to planet scores. You may be able to use the chart on this page, or you can devise one of your own.

6. Your class needs to decide how fancy you want your Olympic games to be. Your planet teams could design uniforms, flags, or even write the lyrics to planetary anthems that will represent your "home."

7. On the day of the Solar System Olympics, set up your contests, grab your pencils, and let the games begin!

 ## Digging Deeper

- What features other than gravity would contribute to designing some Olympic events on another planet?

An astronaut from the Apollo space program on the Moon.

- How would you set up an Olympic event in your classroom? Where will the stations be placed? Will everyone compete in every event, or will athletes need to choose their events? How much time will you need for planning? How long will the Olympics take?

IN YOUR JOURNAL

In "The Lunar Olympics," Einstein knew that even though the Moon's gravity is one-sixth that of Earth, a high jumper wouldn't really jump six times higher. Read Einstein's solution, and then see if you can write a formula to calculate jumping events.

READ MORE ABOUT IT

You might get some good ideas for this activity from books or articles about the Olympics. *The Olympic Summer Games,* by Caroline Arnold (Watts, 1991), is useful because it lists and describes events. Other books focus on one particular Olympic sport, such as gymnastics. Browse in both the children's and adult sections of the library in the area marked 796.480.

SOLAR SYSTEM OLYMPICS

OLYMPIC EVENT	PLANET	SURFACE GRAVITY	EARTH RESULTS	CONVERSION EQUATION	PLANET RESULTS

SURFACE GRAVITY OF THE PLANETS*

Mercury	$4/10$ or .4	Saturn	$1 1/10$ or 1.1
Venus	$9/10$ or .9	Uranus	$1 2/10$ or 1.2
Mars	$4/10$ or .4	Neptune	$1 2/10$ or 1.2
Jupiter	$2 6/10$ or 2.6	Pluto	$1/10$ or .1

*For more accurate results, use the more detailed surface gravity figures in the chart on pages 34–35.

Stellar Time Line

What can we learn about the life of the Sun by studying other stars? In this activity you will make a time line of the events in an average star's life and see what's in store for our neighborhood star.

 YOU WILL NEED

☐ books on the Sun and stars
☐ markers and paper

 PROCEDURE

1. Read through several books about the Sun and stars. Make notes of the events in the birth, life, and death of stars.

2. Use the information from books and encyclopedias to make a time line of the life and death of stars.

Here are some of the major categories you will want to include on your time line. (You will need to chart the lives of average, large, and very large stars.)

AVERAGE	LARGE	VERY LARGE
1. Birth of star	1. Birth of star	1. Birth of star
2. Stable star	2. Stable star	2. Stable star
3. Red giant	3. Red giant	3. Red giant
4. White dwarf	4. Supernova	4. Supernova
5. Nova	5. Neutron star	5. Black hole
6. Black dwarf	6. Pulsar	

3. Use your books to collect additional data on the stars. Include on your time line the approximate years, sizes, temperatures, and colors at each stage.

4. After you have completed your time line, hang the names of stars and star clusters in their proper places on the time line. Here are a few to get you started.

- **The Sun** is considered middle-aged. Indicate its position on your time line. Do some research to find out which path it will eventually follow.

- **The Pleiades,** a star cluster in the constellation Taurus, is a "stellar nursery." The stars in this cluster are so young, some of the gas and dust from which they were born can still be seen.
- **Betelgeuse,** the star that marks the left shoulder of Orion, is a red giant. You can see its red color with your naked eye.

 DIGGING DEEPER

- It is hard to do hands-on experiments with stars, so you will need to do a lot of reading to learn more about them. Check out newspapers and astronomy magazines for the latest information received from telescopes and space probes. Share some interesting research with your classmates.
- The Pleiades fall close to the beginning of your time line, but they've been around for close to 50 million years. Look for some of the ancient folklore about these young stars.
- Take a look at a few of the rare recordings of some stars' explosive deaths (don't forget to place them on your time line):

  ○ The Crab nebula—remnants of a supernova observed on Earth in A.D. 1054 (*Stars*).
  ○ The Tarantula nebula and the most recently observed supernova in our galaxy, Supernova 1987A (*Galaxies*).

 IN YOUR JOURNAL

Are black dwarfs, neutron stars, and pulsars the end of stars? Not really. The energy, gases, and matter scattered by red giants and supernovas travel through space, then re-form into new stars.

Can you find a way to remake your time line into a "time circle"?

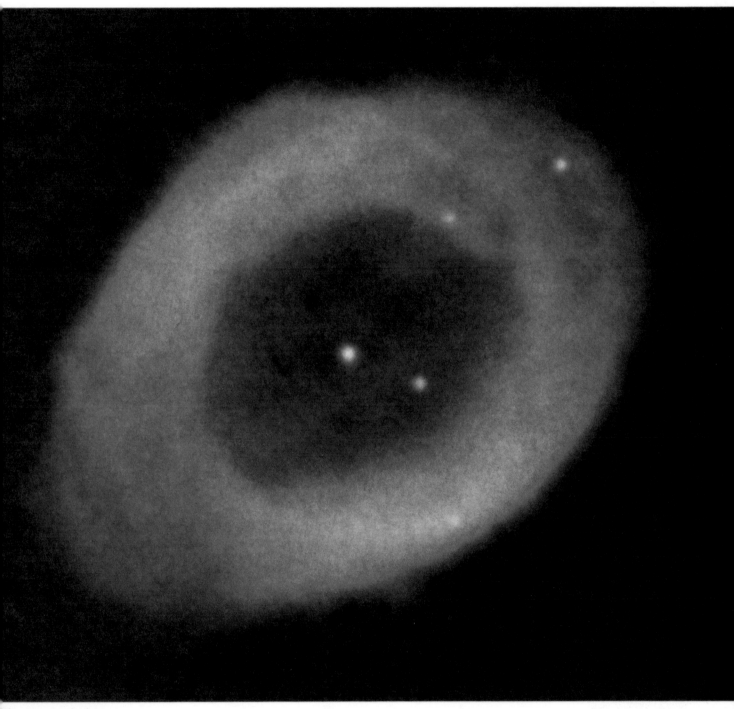

The Ring nebula.

READ MORE ABOUT IT

A time line is a quasimathematical description of space. There are many other ways, including poetry, to explore human interest in, and appreciation of, astronomy.

Read the poetry of Myra Cohn Livingston in *Space Songs* (Holiday House, 1988). Perhaps you and your classmates can compile your own anthology of astronomy poems by looking in other poetry books. What about adding your own space poetry to the collection?

In the Blink of a Star

In 1967, astronomers were baffled by some unexplained bursts of radio waves traveling through space. After you read about pulsars and complete the activities below, you will have a better idea of what was really going on.

 YOU WILL NEED

☐ books with information on pulsars and neutron stars
☐ a flashlight
☐ about 24 inches of string or fishing line
☐ a weight, such as a fishing weight, that can be secured onto the string
☐ a wooden spool

 PROCEDURE

1. Before you begin, you might want to read about pulsars—the culprits behind the mystery. Fact:

- In their final stages, some of the largest stars in the universe collapse, creating neutron stars. These stars can be as small as ten miles in diameter.
- Neutron stars rotate much faster than their larger ancestors—up to thirty times a second!
- Neutron stars give off a beam of X-ray radiation. As the neutron stars rotate, these beams sweep across space, much like the light of a lighthouse. When detected, they seem to blink, or pulse, and are referred to as pulsars.

2. You can demonstrate why the X rays appear in bursts with a flashlight in a darkened room. The light from the flashlight represents the radiation beaming from the pulsar.

- Have one student, acting as the pulsar, hold a flashlight. The light must be pointing directly away from his or her body.
- With the flashlight turned on, have the "pulsar" rotate slowly.
- Can you use the beam of light to explain why pulsars appear to blink?

3. After their collapse, neutron stars rotate very rapidly. Their mass (weight) is squeezed into a much smaller size.

Try this activity to demonstrate how objects rotate faster when their size decreases but their weight remains the same.

- Firmly attach the weight to one end of the string or fishing line. (Make sure it's on tight to avoid accidents.)
- Insert the other end of the string through the spool.
- Holding the spool in one hand and the bottom of the string in the other, spin the weight in a large circle above the spool.
- Slowly pull the string down through the spool to decrease the diameter of the weight's revolution.
- As the diameter of the revolution gets smaller, what happens to the speed of the weight's rotation?

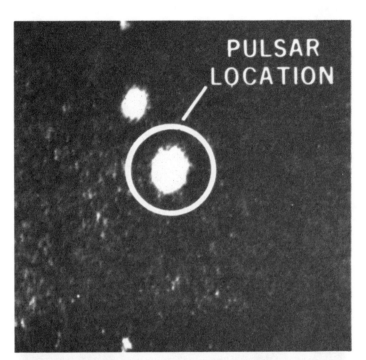

PULSAR
LOCATION

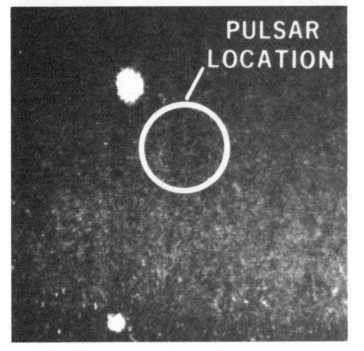

PULSAR
LOCATION

The Crab nebula pulsar.

 DIGGING DEEPER

- Find an X-ray photograph of a pulsar, such as the Crab nebula's pulsar illustrated here. How did your flashlight "pulsar" help explain why the pulsar appears to blink?
- Picture a figure skater spinning faster and faster until she is just a blur. What does she do with her arms as her speed increases? How is this similar to the rotation of a star that collapses down to a tiny neutron star?

 IN YOUR JOURNAL

At first, astronomers jokingly blamed the mystery pulses on "Little Green Men," and before long, these bursts were known as LGMs. Write a short story about a mysterious discovery from space.

 READ MORE ABOUT IT

It takes both information and imagination to figure out what's really happening in space when astronomers can't visit and see for themselves. Locate a biography of an astronomer and describe what she or he saw from Earth. (For a list of astronomers see page 85.) How did the astronomer figure out what was *really* happening? How did she or he convince others?

Black Holes in Space

Black holes may sound like science fiction, but scientists believe they really exist. Try making this model of these space mysteries.

 YOU WILL NEED

- ☐ books with information on black holes
- ☐ a large piece of dark fabric or felt, about 36 inches square
- ☐ many sets of hands to stretch the fabric tight and level
- ☐ a hand-held vacuum cleaner with hose attachment
- ☐ sand, rice, or some other small-grained substance

 PROCEDURE

1. Read about the stars known as black holes. Scientists believe that the gravitational pull of a black hole is so strong, nothing can escape it, not even light. You can model these stars by using sand to represent light and the suction of a vacuum to represent the gravity of a black hole. *Don't forget to use your vacuum cleaner to clean up any spills.*

2. Stretch the fabric level, several feet above the floor. To keep the fabric as level as possible, perhaps you could rest your arms on desks that have been arranged in a circle.

3. Choose one person to lie underneath the fabric and hold the vacuum hose against the center of the fabric.
The people holding the edges will have to hold the fabric tightly so that it doesn't get sucked in when the vacuum is turned on. If the fabric begins to get sucked into the hose, turn off and unplug the vacuum cleaner immediately. If necessary, have an adult help you remove the fabric.

4. Place a handful of sand on the outer edges of the stretched fabric.

5. Turn on the vacuum. What happens to the sand?

6. Sprinkle sand closer to the "black hole." How close to the hole can you sprinkle the sand and not have it sucked into the center? Remember that what you have made is only a model. It is the gravitational field of a black hole that would prevent light from escaping.

 DIGGING DEEPER

In a book of spectacular photographs *(Stars),* Seymour Simon has chosen a drawing to illustrate a black hole. Why? Do you think any photographs of black holes exist? Why or why not?

 IN YOUR JOURNAL and **READ MORE ABOUT IT**

Some books about black holes, such as Franklyn M. Branley's *Journey into a Black Hole* (Harper & Row, 1986), are written for young children. Others, like *Quasars, Pulsars and Black Holes,* by Melvin Berger (Putnam, 1977), or *Quasars, Pulsars and Black Holes in Space,* by Isaac Asimov (Gareth Stevens, 1988), are written for older readers. Think about what in a book makes the publisher or author say it's for younger or older children. Is it just the *amount* of information included?

Red Giant Puzzles

What happens to stars as they get hotter and hotter? This activity might help you understand what occurs as stars enter the red-giant phase.

 YOU WILL NEED

- ☐ a 2-liter plastic soda bottle, cooled in the refrigerator
- ☐ balloons
- ☐ a pan of very warm water

 PROCEDURE

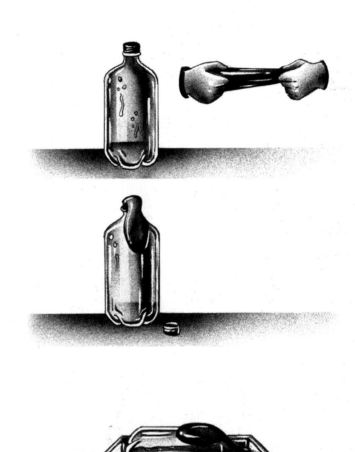

1. In his book *Stars*, Seymour Simon explains that when stars begin burning hotter and hotter after about ten billion years, they balloon out, "like a piece of popcorn when it 'pops.'"

2. You can demonstrate why the outer gases "balloon" when the star gets hotter by warming the air in a soda bottle.
Leave a tightly sealed empty soda bottle in the refrigerator for at least one hour.

3. Take the bottle out of the refrigerator and immediately replace the cap with an uninflated (but previously stretched) balloon. Make sure the balloon is secured on the neck of the bottle.

4. Place the soda bottle in a pan of very warm water in a warm spot in your room.

 DIGGING DEEPER

- What happens to the balloon as the bottle's contents get warmer and warmer?
- How does this help to explain what happens to the gases surrounding a star that is getting hotter and hotter?
- Read more about red supergiants and red giants, like Betelgeuse, a star that is 250 million miles across.

IN YOUR JOURNAL and READ MORE ABOUT IT

Some people prefer to read about a topic like red giants before seeing a demonstration. Others prefer to see the demonstration first. Which do you prefer? Why?

Constellation Theater

Throughout history, people have developed legends and stories to match the nightly picture shows in the sky. Make the star cans on this page and create a star-and-story show of your own.

 YOU WILL NEED

- ☐ books about constellations
- ☐ a pencil and tracing paper
- ☐ tape
- ☐ an empty coffee can or oatmeal box
- ☐ a hammer
- ☐ nails
- ☐ a flashlight
- ☐ a sock

  (and you may want to use a photocopying machine that can reduce and enlarge)

▶ **PROCEDURE**

1. Browse through several books about constellations. Choose one constellation and read some of the myths and legends surrounding it. Compare the myths of different cultures. Learn when and where your constellation can be seen in the sky.

2. Using an illustration from one of the books, trace a pattern of one constellation. Sample patterns are included here. Your pattern should have dots representing the major stars in the constellation, and it should be about 4 inches in diameter. You may have to reduce or enlarge your pattern. If one is available, use a photocopying machine that reduces and enlarges images.

3. Tape the 4-inch pattern to the end of a coffee can or oatmeal box.

4. Use the hammer and a nail to pierce holes through the dots in the pattern and through the can underneath.

Before you remove the pattern, think about how you want your finished constellation to shine. Are all the stars in a star group the same size? Are they the same color? How can you make your stars appear like the real stars?

5. Drop the flashlight into the sock and secure the sock opening around the open end of the can. (This will help keep the light from scattering outside of the can. You can still feel for the flashlight's switch through the sock.)

6. Produce a classroom "constellation theater" with the other students in the class. Take turns shining your constellations on the ceiling or wall of your darkened room. When it is your turn to display your star show, tell a legend about your constellation.

7. You might prefer to reproduce your constellations on black paper with luminescent paint. Hang your finished products horizontally from the ceiling and "charge" the paint with a flashlight. Lean back and enjoy some indoor stargazing.

 DIGGING DEEPER

- How many legends did your class find for any one constellation? How are these legends the same? How are they different?
- Make up some new characters and legends that fit the star patterns of your constellations. What mythical heroes do we have today that lend themselves to your starry pictures?
- It's interesting to think that the stars we see in the twentieth century are the same ones seen by all people who have lived on Earth. How does our increased understanding of the stars and universe affect our modern stories?

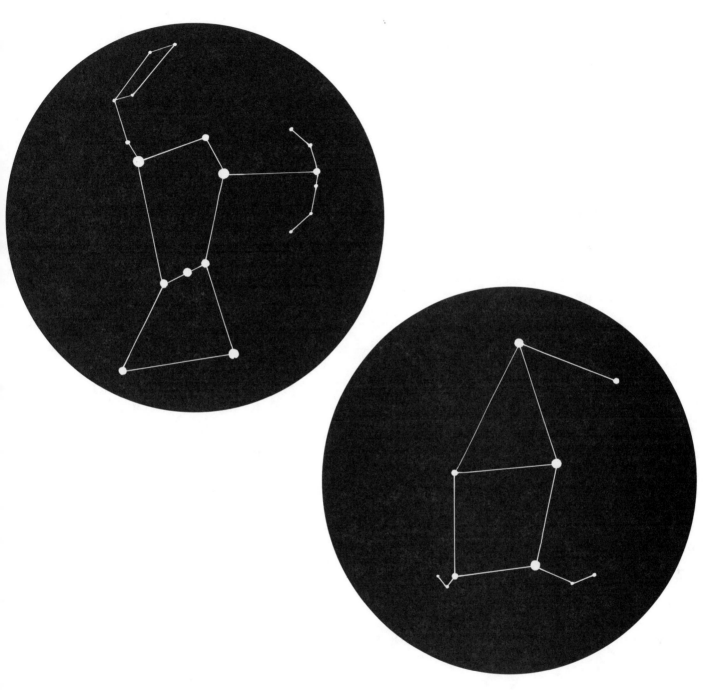

  IN YOUR JOURNAL and
READ MORE ABOUT IT

After reading several stories that explain the origins of the constellations, write one of your own. The following might prove helpful: *The Constellations: How They Came to Be,* by Roy A. Gallant (Four Winds/Macmillan, 1991); *What's in the Names of Stars and Constellations,* by Peter Limburg (Coward, McCann, 1976); *The Heavenly Zoo: Legends and Tales of the Stars,* retold in a lyric voice by Alison Lurie (Farrar, Strauss and Giroux, 1979); and *365 Starry Nights: An Introduction to Astronomy for Every Night of the Year,* by Chet Raymo (Prentice Hall, 1982).

Pictures in the Sky

You may be familiar with the belt, shoulder, and sword of the constellation Orion, or the simple handles and bowls of the Big and Little Dippers. There are at least eighty-five other constellations in the night sky. See how many you can locate.

 YOU WILL NEED

- [ ] constellation books with star maps
- [ ] **Starry-Night Flashlight** (directions on the next page)
- [ ] warm clothes for chilly nights
- [ ] a cloudless night

 PROCEDURE

1. Locate books about constellations and choose several formations you would like to find in the night sky. The books will tell you which are the easiest to locate.

2. Locate a star map in the book. Your chart should be clearly labeled with the dates and times of day it represents. Because the Earth revolves around the Sun, a sky at nine o'clock at night looks different in March from the way it does in April, May, or any other month.

3. Find a location as far from any light pollution as possible. If you are not going with a parent, make sure an adult knows where you will be. Do not go to a new location without permission.

4. Give your eyes about fifteen minutes to adjust to the dark. Careful! Even after a brief glimpse of white light, your eyes will need to readjust to the night. You may want to make the **Starry-Night Flashlight** so you can walk around safely and read your star charts.

5. Enjoy. Viewing constellations is like visiting a museum in the sky, for you are looking at the same stars, in much the same patterns, as every person who has ever lived on this Earth. Learning the stories and beliefs associated with the constellations can help you better understand those who have lived before us.

 IN YOUR JOURNAL and READ MORE ABOUT IT

Choose a culture to investigate. For example, readers interested in Native American culture might find useful books like *Star Tales: North American Indian Stories about the Stars,* by Gretchen Will Mayo (Walker, 1987), or *The Star Gazers,* by Christine Widman (HarperCollins, 1989). Read about how the culture you have chosen named or kept track of the stars. Think about how the star stories they told reflect what was or is important to them—their survival, their hopes, their dreams. Retell one of these stories as a grandparent would tell it to her or his grandchild.

Starry-Night Flashlight

*How can you read your star charts, take notes on what you are seeing, or even check your watch once your eyes have adjusted to the dark of night? Make this **Starry-Night Flashlight** to use on your next stargazing adventure.*

 YOU WILL NEED

- ☐ an ordinary flashlight
- ☐ red cellophane or brown paper
- ☐ a paper-towel tube or piece of heavy paper

 PROCEDURE

1. Unscrew the top of an ordinary flashlight.

2. Insert a piece of red cellophane or two layers of brown paper under the glass.

3. Reassemble the flashlight.

4. You will cut down on scattered light if you tape a cardboard tube (or a tube of rolled paper) to the end of the flashlight. Cut the end of the tube at a 45-degree angle to get the maximum amount of concentrated light.

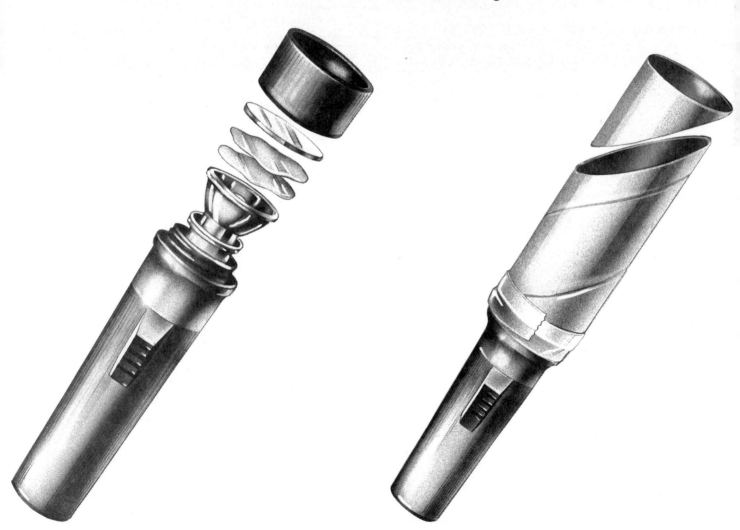

Family Stargazing

Have you ever stood quietly and just looked up at the night sky? Give it a try with a friend or a member of your family. You just might want to make this a regular activity. Remember, whenever you go stargazing, make sure that you are accompanied by an adult or that you let an adult know where you are going and when you will return.

 YOU WILL NEED

- ☐ books with star charts
- ☐ a cloudless night (preferably with no Moon)
- ☐ a location as far from city lights as possible
- ☐ binoculars or a telescope (optional)
- ☐ warm clothes for chilly nights

 PROCEDURE

1. Choose a place with very little light pollution, as far from street- and house lights as possible. If you do this on a moonless night, or on an evening with a thin crescent Moon, you will have little interference from natural light.

2. Look at the big sky. What do you see? Turn slowly and take in the view from all directions. Give your eyes plenty of time to adapt to the darkness of the evening. (You might want to make the **Starry-Night Flashlight** on page 63 to take with you.) Can you see more stars after you've been out for fifteen minutes?

3. Ask yourself, does every section of the sky look the same? What differences can you see?

4. Take a closer look. Are the stars grouped together? Do you recognize any constellation patterns? Can you make any patterns of your own?

5. Look closer still and examine some stars one by one. Are they all the same? Do they *all* twinkle? Are they the same size? Are they the same color?

6. If you have binoculars or a telescope, take an even closer look. What do you see?

 DIGGING DEEPER

- Talk about your stargazing experience. What did you notice on this night that you had never noticed before?
- Ask your parents or grandparents to tell you some starry memories. Did they stargaze when they were young? Have they ever seen a shooting star, a comet, or the northern lights? Did they ever watch an eclipse of the Moon?

 IN YOUR JOURNAL and **READ MORE ABOUT IT**

With your family, read Jane Yolen's *Owl Moon* (Putnam, 1987) or Anna Grossnickle Hines's *Sky All Around* (Clarion, 1989). How are these families the same or different from your own? As you recall your own excursion out-of-doors, think about the stories you will want to tell your own children about observing the night sky. Write one down to help yourself remember.

Pointing to Polaris

Could you travel north without a compass or map? After trying this activity on the next clear night, you will discover a set of "pointers" that will mark the way.

 YOU WILL NEED

☐ a clear night in the northern hemisphere
☐ a book or star map to help you find the Big Dipper

PROCEDURE

1. With the help of a book or star map, locate the Big Dipper, a group of seven stars in the shape of a dipper, or large ladle.

2. Find the bowl of the dipper, and then identify the two stars on the outer edge of the bowl, opposite the handle. Extend an imaginary line up through these two stars—this will lead to Polaris, the North Star.

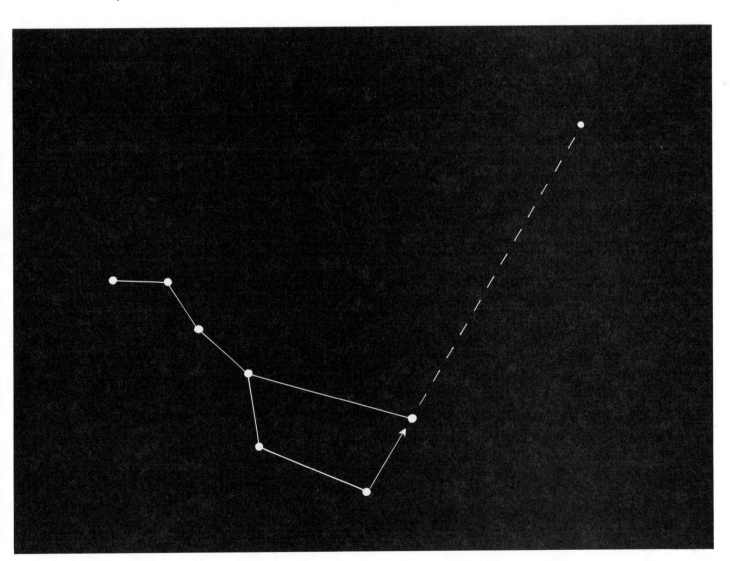

Canopy of Stars

Look up at the sky tonight and notice how it appears like a painted dome above your head. If you look again in several hours, you should see that our dome appears to move, ever so slowly. Try this activity to demonstrate the apparent movement of the stars—and show how one star never seems to move.

 YOU WILL NEED

- [ ] books about constellations that include star maps
- [ ] a solid-color umbrella (one that will not be needed again)
- [ ] white or luminescent paint

 PROCEDURE

Demonstrate the rising and setting of the stars, as well as their movement around Polaris, the North Star, with an old umbrella and some paint.

1. Use the center point of the umbrella, where the handle intersects with the fabric, to represent Polaris, the star located above the north pole.

2. Position and paint the Big Dipper on the inside of the opened umbrella so that its pointer stars point to Polaris. (See **Pointing to Polaris,** page 65.)

3. Use books and star maps to help you position and paint other constellations on your night-sky umbrella.

4. After the paint has dried, rest the handle of the umbrella on a stool or some books stacked on a table. The tabletop will represent the horizon.

5. If the point of the umbrella represents north, figure out which side of the table will represent east and which side will be west.

6. Viewed from above the north pole, the Earth rotates counterclockwise. Think carefully to determine in which direction you will need to rotate the umbrella to mimic the apparent movement of the stars.

7. You might want to take note of how high in the sky Polaris appears. See if you can angle your umbrella so that your Polaris appears at the same height above your tabletop horizon.

8. Watch what happens to the Big Dipper as it moves around Polaris. Does it fall below the horizon? Would it point to the North Star at any time of night, any time of the year?

 DIGGING DEEPER

- Picture an imaginary line extending through the center of the Earth from south pole to north pole and on up into space. It would eventually intersect with Polaris, the North Star. If you were to travel to the north pole, lie on your back, and look up at the sky, what star would be directly over your head? How would the stars appear as the Earth rotated on its axis?
- Use books and your umbrella to discuss the movement and location of the Big Dipper, the Little Dipper, Draco, Cassiopeia, and Cepheus. These constellations are called circumpolar. As you might guess from the root words, *circumpolar* means "to circle the pole."

 IN YOUR JOURNAL

In the 1800s people escaping slavery found their way north by following "the drinking gourd." Their drinking gourd was the Big Dipper, and it pointed directly to the North Star. What were some of the advantages and disadvantages to using stars as a guide?

Some of the millions and millions of stars in the Milky Way.

 ### READ MORE ABOUT IT

Stars have been important for families for many reasons. To see how a knowledge of the night sky actually saved people's lives, read *Follow the Drinking Gourd,* by Jeanette Winter (Knopf, 1988); *The Drinking Gourd,* by F. N. Monjo (Harper & Row, 1970); or *Carry On, Mr. Bowditch,* by Jean Lee Latham (Houghton Mifflin, 1955).

Recording Star Trails

Have you ever seen photographs of the circular patterns made by stars over several hours? These are called circumpolar trails. If you have a camera with a manually operated shutter, you can take pictures of these starry trails.

You Will Need

- ☐ illustrations showing circumpolar trails (circular tracks of stars around Polaris)
- ☐ a 35-millimeter camera with a manual shutter that can be set for time exposure
- ☐ locking cable release (allows you to keep the shutter open without touching the camera)
- ☐ a tripod
- ☐ color or black-and-white film (as "fast" as possible—speeds of ISO 400 to 1,000)
- ☐ pocket notebook
- ☐ at least one hour of time on a clear night
- ☐ the assistance of someone who knows how to operate the camera

 Procedure

1. Look through books for long-exposure photographs of the stars circling Polaris, the North Star. (See the one at right, as well as the one in Seymour Simon's *The Long View into Space*.) Read the captions and text to see how the author explains these unusual pictures of the night sky. Then try taking your own photograph of star trails with a 35-millimeter manually operated camera.

2. Attach the cable release to the camera, and then secure the loaded camera to a tripod.

3. If your camera has an adjustable depth of field, place it on infinity: ∞.

4. Set the aperture (f-stop) to the lowest number, probably f-2 or f-2.8. (The lowest number is the largest opening and will let in the most light.)

5. Point the camera directly at Polaris, the North Star. (See the **Pointing to Polaris** activity, page 65.)

6. Open the shutter with the cable release and leave it open for at least one hour.

7. You may need to practice with several rolls of film before you get a good picture of the stars' movement. In your notebook, keep track of the details of each picture—time of night, moonlight, weather conditions, frame number, camera setting, and length of time you kept the shutter open.

8. Experiment with your photographs. How does changing the exposure time (length of time the shutter is open) affect your pictures?

Digging Deeper

- Compare your photographs with those you find in books and magazines.

  - ○ Did you get as many star trails? What might affect the number of star trails you record on film?
  - ○ Are your trails longer or shorter than those in the book? What might affect the length of star trails recorded on film?

- What would happen if you did not point the camera at the North Star?

Circumpolar trails, as captured in a long-exposure photograph.

 ### IN YOUR JOURNAL

Look at a picture you took of star trails or at a photograph in a book. If the Earth was not rotating, what would these long-exposure photographs look like?

 ### READ MORE ABOUT IT

For more information on photographing the stars and planets, see Robert Little's *Astrophotography: A Step-by-Step Approach* (Macmillan, 1986).

Living in Space

What would be the thrills and dangers of living in space? What would be the demands? Design your own space station that meets the many challenges of life without any outside sources of oxygen, water, or television.

 YOU WILL NEED

☐ books on space stations, planets, and space
☐ poster board and markers or other materials to make a model
☐ imagination

 PROCEDURE

1. As a class, list the things you need to maintain human life. Then add items and events that make life comfortable. Finally, brainstorm a list of what makes life enjoyable.

2. Choose a location at which you would like to base a space station. It could be

- orbiting above the Earth,
- based on a planet or moon,
- traveling through or beyond the Solar System.

On your own, or with a partner who has chosen the same location, design a space station for the future.

3. Before you begin, decide on your space station's function. Why are you putting a station in space?

- Is it a zero-gravity laboratory?
- Will it be the first human colony on the Moon or Mars?
- Will it follow the path of a comet or study the asteroid belt?
- Is it a stop-off and repair facility for other spaceships?

4. Collect information from encyclopedias, astronomy magazines, and books about the planets, Solar System, comets, meteors, and asteroids. What challenges will your mission face?

5. Use your list of human needs (from step 1), your mission objectives, and what you learned about your location in space to plan a successful mission.

6. Design a blueprint or model of your space station. Show how your inhabitants will get oxygen, food, and water; where they will sleep, eat, work, and play; and how they will move around within the station or on trips outside the station.

 DIGGING DEEPER

Make a sealed terrarium in a jar. What is happening to the moisture, oxygen, and carbon dioxide inside the jar? See how long you can keep plants growing. Are there other forms of life that can stay alive in the terrarium—ants, grasshoppers, worms? Do you believe it is ethical to experiment with living creatures?

 IN YOUR JOURNAL

Observe your sealed terrarium closely. How do your plants look? Where is moisture collecting? Does it look different on warmer and colder days? Use a page of your journal to record daily observations for two weeks.

 READ MORE ABOUT IT

In "Are You Ready for Space?"—an activity in *How to Be a Space Scientist in Your Own Home*—Seymour Simon discusses some of the hardships of living in space—crowded conditions, boredom, and no sensation of day and night, just to name a few.

The Magellan *space probe, which orbited Venus in 1990. Earth is in the background.*

- What books would you bring along for entertainment or information?
- What books would you write while there?

 SEYMOUR SAYS

I've written over a hundred books, and when someone asks me which is my favorite, it's like asking a parent who has a hundred kids, "Who's your favorite kid?" If I told you my favorite book, my other books would attack me.

The truth is, I do have favorites, but they're always changing. My favorite books are the next books I'm going to write. Not the one I'm writing now, because that's hard work. It's the ones after the one I'm writing now, because they're so exciting for me to think about.

Pixel Perfect

Did you know that every planet except Pluto has had visits from spacecraft? None of the spacecraft have returned to Earth, but each has sent back data for astronomers to share with the world. Complete this activity to get an idea of how these pictures are transmitted.

 YOU WILL NEED

☐ a partner
☐ a pencil for each partner
☐ graph paper for each partner

 PROCEDURE

Spacecraft cannot mail photographs to Earth. Instead, they change, or convert, the pictures into many tiny squares, called pixels. Each pixel is assigned a number that represents how bright or dark it is. The numbers are sent to Earth through radio signals and then turned back into a picture.

You can try a transmission similar to those sent from space. It will take two people—a transmitter and a receiver.

1. Both partners should label their paper in exactly the same way. Starting with 1, write one number in each square down the left side of the page. Starting with the letter A, write one letter in each square across the top of the page. (Leave the top left square blank.)

You can now identify each square by its position. Reading left to right, the first square will be called A-1, the next will be B-1, the next will be C-1, and so on. These squares are like the pixels that make up an image from space.

2. The transmitter should draw a black-and-white picture on his or her graph paper, making sure each square is either totally filled or totally empty. Do not show the picture to the receiver.

3. Following along from left to right, the transmitter and the receiver will now "scan" the picture. Start with the first square in row 1 and move across that row to the right. For each box, the transmitter will say "0" for a white box, "1" for a black box.

KEY: 0 = white   1 = black

RECEIVER: Call out the first box by saying, "A-1."

TRANSMITTER: Respond with "0" if your A-1 box is white, or "1" if your A-1 box is black.

RECEIVER: If you hear "0," leave your A-1 box empty. If you hear "1," color in the box.

RECEIVER: Call out the second box by saying, "B-1."

TRANSMITTER: Respond with a "0" or "1" to let the receiver know whether your B-1 box is white or black.

4. Repeat this procedure for each row until you have scanned the entire page.

 DIGGING DEEPER

- When you have finished the page, compare your pictures. How well did you communicate with each other? Can you make your transmission clearer?
- Were you happy with the detail of your pictures? How would using graph paper with larger or smaller squares affect the quality of your picture?

 IN YOUR JOURNAL and READ MORE ABOUT IT

Look at *Get the Message,* by Gloria Skurzynski (Bradbury, 1993), or another book that describes modern communication. In your journal describe or diagram how messages are transmitted via satellite. You might want to design a means of sending a beam of light around the room using mirrors.

A Sharper Image

(Note: You may want to complete **Pixel Perfect** on page 72 before you do this activity.)

Pictures from modern spacecraft may contain as many as 2.5 million pixels, each of which is assigned one of 256 numbers showing how bright or dark it is! It's probably not possible for you to make a picture like that, but you can make a fairly detailed picture by completing this activity.

 YOU WILL NEED

☐ a partner
☐ a pencil for each partner
☐ graph paper for each partner

 PROCEDURE

Rather than using 0 for white and 1 for black, scientists have developed a gray scale, which uses the numbers 0 to 255—0 is white, 255 is black, and the numbers in between represent shades of gray.

1. Look at your picture from the **Pixel Perfect** activity. You can make a more detailed picture by using a gray scale of 0 to 3. Zero will be white, and 3 will be black. Assign a light gray to number 1 and a darker gray to number 2.

2. It's important that the transmitter and receiver use the same shade of gray for each number, so the two of you will need to find a way to keep your grays constant. Complete the color key on this page and keep it where both of you can refer to it.

3. Label your graph papers as you did in the **Pixel Perfect** activity. Starting with 1, write one number in each square down the left side of the page. Starting with the letter A, write one letter in each square across the top of the page. (Note: Using graph paper with more squares to the inch will allow you to transmit a more detailed picture.)

4. The transmitter should draw a detailed picture on his or her graph paper, making sure each square is white, light gray, dark gray, or black. Do not show the picture to the receiver.

5. Scan the picture as you did in **Pixel Perfect,** moving from left to right, one row at a time. For each box, the transmitter will say "0" for white, "1" for light gray, "2" for dark gray, and "3" for black. The receiver will color in the square according to the number transmitted.

6. Repeat until the entire picture has been transmitted.

 DIGGING DEEPER

• Compare the detail of your pictures in this activity with those you made in **Pixel Perfect.**
• You may want to try your transmission using a 0 to 7, or an even more detailed, gray scale. However, it will be more difficult to control the shades of gray. You might use a series of X's (one X for 1, two crossed X's for 2, three crossed X's for 3, and so on). What other strategies could you use?

 READ MORE ABOUT IT

Use a good magnifying glass to look at photographs in a newspaper or pictures in a book. How many pixels per half-inch square do you see? Is there a relationship between the number of pixels and the quality of the print?

GRAY SCALE KEY

Fill in the boxes with the shades of gray for each number. Remember to make 0 white and 3 black.

0	1	2	3

Moving Through Space

Question: Are you sitting still right now?
Answer: Well, you might be sitting, but you are definitely not still.
This activity will help you demonstrate the many directions in which your little piece of planet Earth is traveling at this very moment.

 YOU WILL NEED

- ☐ a very large area—a gym, field, or empty parking lot
- ☐ your entire class

 PROCEDURE

1. The four movements the Earth makes every second in time are Earth's rotation, Earth's revolution around the Sun, the rotation of our Galaxy, and the expansion of the universe. Before you begin, assign these roles to the students in your class:

Sun . . . . one person
Earth . . . . one person (at a time)
Milky Way galaxy . . . . several people
Other galaxies . . . . several *groups* of people

2. The Earth rotates on its axis once each day. To demonstrate this, the person representing Earth should turn around once, in place.

3. The Earth revolves around the Sun once each year. Have "Earth" travel in a circle around the "Sun." Don't forget to keep rotating! (This will be a dizzying experience. You may want to have alternate Earths take turns revolving around the Sun.)

4. Position the Earth and Sun into the spinning Milky Way galaxy. Although the Solar System is traveling at a speed of 600 thousand miles per hour, your Milky Way won't have to move *too* fast. It takes 225 million years to complete one rotation.

5. Like the spots on an inflating balloon, all the galaxies in the universe are moving farther and farther away from one another. (See **The Expanding Universe,** page 76.) Can you arrange your galaxies to expand through your open space?

6. After you have mastered your dance, try adding other planets, moons, comets, and the asteroid belt.

 DIGGING DEEPER

- Use illustrations in books (including the one at right) to locate our planet's position within the Solar System and the Milky Way. Would our speed through the Milky Way be faster or slower if we were closer to the center of the Galaxy?
- Read about Mercury's rate of rotation and revolution. (Its rotation takes fifty-nine Earth days, and its revolution takes eighty-eight Earth days.) Demonstrate or describe how its movement would compare to Earth's.

 IN YOUR JOURNAL

Record your address the way Seymour Simon describes below.

 SEYMOUR SAYS

In the third grade, I became interested in where I was located in space, and then I learned the perfect way to set myself down in all this space—by writing my address.

Milky Way Galaxy

Our Solar System

Our Solar System is located in the Milky Way galaxy.

Naturally, when writing your address, you put your name, the street you live on, and the state and zip code. I did all that, but my address kept going. I added the planet Earth. Then I put the group of planets that Earth belongs to—the Solar System. But I wasn't finished, because the Solar System is part of a huge group of stars called the Milky Way galaxy. But I still wasn't finished. The Milky Way galaxy is just one giant group of stars among millions upon millions of other groups of stars that make up the universe. And that was my complete address.

Well, when I was grown up, I wrote a book

called The Long View into Space. *On the last page, I wrote my address, and it went all the way down to the universe. But I guess kids are smarter now than when I was a kid, because I got a letter from a fifth grader. He used my complete address as written in the book, but then he added the zip code of the universe.*

What do you think the perfect zip code for the universe is? Infinity. He didn't write the word, he used the symbol ∞. So make sure you put down the zip code for the universe when you write your complete address.

The Expanding Universe

In 1929, astronomer Edwin Hubble made a startling discovery. All the other galaxies in the universe appeared to be moving away from ours—and the farther away they were, the faster they appeared to be traveling! How could this be?

You can use a balloon to demonstrate Hubble's law—and the expanding universe.

YOU WILL NEED

- ☐ a balloon
- ☐ a marking pen that will write on balloons
- ☐ a flexible tape measure
- ☐ books on galaxies

PROCEDURE

1. With a marking pen, draw several dots on the flat balloon. These dots will represent the galaxies in the universe. You may wish to draw galaxy shapes instead of dots. (Refer to books like *Galaxies* to see the various shapes galaxies form.)

2. Expand your universe by inflating the balloon. Have a classmate hold it tightly, so the air doesn't seep out. What happens to all of the galaxies? Let the air out of the balloon.

3. To demonstrate why distant galaxies would appear to move faster than neighboring galaxies, draw a circle around one dot to represent our Galaxy, the Milky Way. Identify several other galaxies on the balloon with the numbers 1, 2, 3, and so on. Some should be quite close to the Milky Way, some far away.

4. Measure and record the distances between the Milky Way and Galaxy 1, the Milky Way and Galaxy 2, the Milky Way and Galaxy 3, and so on.

5. "Expand" your universe by inflating the balloon and tying a knot. Repeat your measurements between the Milky Way and Galaxies 1, 2, 3, and so on. Record them on your chart.

6. For each pair of galaxies measured, subtract their distances on the flat balloon from their distances on the expanded balloon.

DIGGING DEEPER

- What do you notice about the distances between the galaxies? Do they all move the same distance at the same time? Which pair of galaxies separated the farthest distance?
- Using a balloon to demonstrate the expanding universe shows only the surface of the balloon. Try designing a different expanding universe activity for another group of students. One way to do this is to track the location of raisins in raisin bread when the dough rises and bakes. Can you think of another way to demonstrate in 3-D?

IN YOUR JOURNAL

Here's a real challenge! Knowing that all the other galaxies in the universe are moving away from *us* could lead someone to think that our Galaxy is at the center of the universe. Expand your balloon several times, each time focusing on a different galaxy and how the other galaxies appear to move away from it. Do you think there is a center of the universe? Why?

READ MORE ABOUT IT

Lots of children (and adults) have ideas about space that, upon further investigation, don't hold up. Several books for young people hook readers' interest by focusing on misconceptions. See, for instance, Seymour Simon's *The Dinosaur Is the Biggest Animal That Ever Lived and Other Wrong Ideas You Thought Were True* (Harper & Row, 1984) or *Animal Fact - Animal Fable* (Crown, 1979).

With your classmates, create your own book about commonly held ideas that are really incorrect. Try your book out on other kids, teachers, and parents.

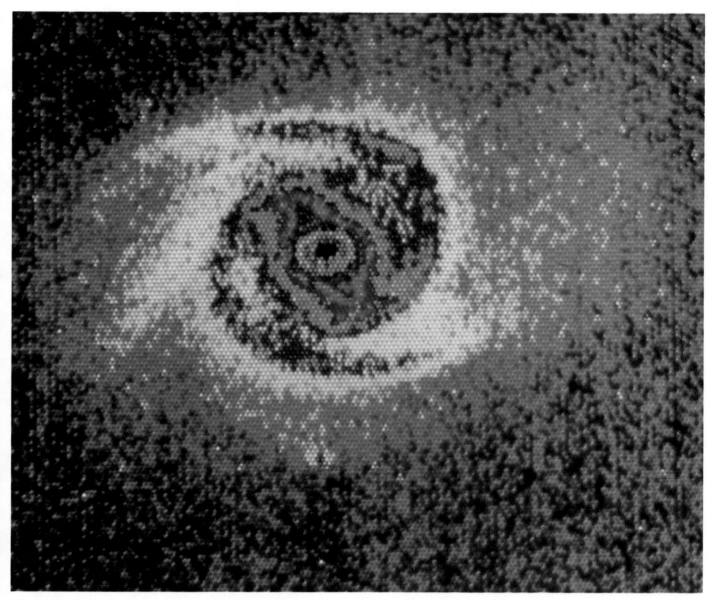

Photo of a barred spiral galaxy, computer-colored to show details.

GALAXY DISTANCES

	MILKY WAY TO GALAXY 1	MILKY WAY TO GALAXY 2	MILKY WAY TO GALAXY 3
Balloon expanded			
Balloon flat			
Distance traveled			

Light-Seconds Away

Riddle: What do our early ancestors and the light from the Andromeda galaxy have in common?
Answer: They're both about two million years old.
Use this activity to discover just how this can be.

YOU WILL NEED

☐ books discussing speed of light, such as *Stars*
☐ a pencil and paper
☐ a calculator
☐ a table of planetary distances

PROCEDURE

1. Light travels at 186,000 miles per second. Astronomers call the distance light travels in one year a *light-year* (almost six trillion miles). Use books like *Stars* to read more about the distances of stars and why they are measured in light-years.

2. You can use a simple mathematical formula to figure out the length of time it would take for light to travel from one place to another.

Formula: *Distance* equals *rate* multiplied by *time.*

> or
> D = RT

In other words, the *distance* to a star or galaxy equals the *rate* of time it takes light to travel (186,000 miles per second) multiplied by the length of *time* it takes the light to get there.

What if you know the distance and the rate, but not the time? Use this formula:

Formula: *Time* equals *distance* divided by *rate.*

> or
> $T = \dfrac{D}{R}$

Example: The Moon is 239,000 miles from Earth. To determine how long it takes *(time)* for the sunlight reflected off the Moon to reach Earth, you would divide the *distance* (239,000 miles) by the *rate* (the speed of light, or 186,000 miles per second).

$$\frac{239,000}{186,000} = 1.28 \text{ seconds}$$

3. Work with a partner to solve these problems:

- How long did the light you are feeling today take to travel to the Earth from the Sun? (The Sun is 93,000,000 miles away.)
- Find a chart with distances from the Sun to the planets (there is one on pages 34–35). Figure out how long it takes for the light of the Sun to reach each planet.
- Our second-closest star (after the Sun) is Alpha Centauri—about 25,000,000,000,000 (trillion) miles away. If you were in a spaceship traveling at the speed of light, how long would it take you to reach that star?

DIGGING DEEPER

- Scientists believe that quasars are billions of light-years away from Earth. This means the light that scientists can detect today actually left the quasar billions of years ago. How could studying this light help scientists uncover some of the mysteries of the universe?
- A light-year *sounds* like it is a measurement of time. How would you explain why it is actually a measurement of distance?

IN YOUR JOURNAL

Write and solve three math problems or riddles that use facts about the speed of light. Exchange problems with a classmate.

Our Solar System is about 30,000 light-years from the center of our Galaxy.

 READ MORE ABOUT IT

Several books try to give readers a sense of how large the biggest numbers really are. Take a look at *How Much Is a Million?*, by David Schwartz (Lothrop, 1985), *Anno's Mysterious Multiplying Jar* (Putnam, 1983), and an intriguing story retold in both *The King's Chessboard*, by David Birch (Dial, 1988), and *A Grain of Rice*, by Helena Claire Pittman (Hastings House, 1986). Are the authors' descriptions effective in giving you a sense of large numbers? How?

Sci-Fi Fun

On October 30, 1938, a popular radio program was interrupted by a news flash—Martians were landing in New Jersey. Many listeners panicked, but little did they know that the announcers were only reading a play, Invasion from Mars, better known as The War of the Worlds, by H. G. Wells.

 YOU WILL NEED

☐ books about the planets
☐ books of science fiction
☐ you may want a copy of *The War of the Worlds,* or a tape of the radio play that tricked the nation, *Invasion from Mars.*

 PROCEDURE

1. The panic is not so surprising when you understand that people used to think intelligent life existed on Mars. Seymour Simon explains why.

There was one astronomer who spent his entire adult life studying Mars. He began to think that he saw something on the surface of Mars—straight lines crisscrossing each other. He knew that there were very few straight lines in nature.

He looked at the lines and said to himself, What could these lines be? He knew that rivers would appear crooked, so he decided they must be canals. But canals aren't formed by nature—they are made by someone or something. Therefore, he reasoned, there had to be Martians to make them.

Years later, we sent the Viking spacecraft to Mars. When it got close enough to send back pictures of the Martian surface, we saw craters, giant volcanoes, even a valley four times deeper and longer than the Grand Canyon—but not a single canal.

Did this prove that there are no Martians? No, but it proved that there are no Martians that like to build canals.

By the way, on orders from Earth, Viking ran tests and collected samples from the soil and air. It did not detect a trace of life on Mars. That doesn't mean that there is no life on Mars, but we haven't found any yet. What a shame.

2. With a partner, discuss whether or not you would have believed the radio broadcast of *Invasion from Mars.* Then make a list of story elements that would have made the play believable to you. (If possible, listen to a portion of the broadcast on tape, or read the play.)

3. With your partner or on your own, write a radio play or TV script that describes an alien visit to Earth. As you write, think about these issues:

- People in the 1990s are better informed about space than people were in 1938. How will you convince them that your aliens are real?
- Be able to describe the planet your aliens come from. Talk about its sun(s), moon(s), atmosphere, ring(s), and surface characteristics.
- How will the features of the planet affect your alien's appearance and ability to adjust to Earth?
- How will the aliens and humans communicate? What common signs or symbols might they share?

4. If you'd rather, write a play about a human voyage to another planet.

 DIGGING DEEPER

- Do you think it is right for science fiction to be broadcast as a news event?
- How does scriptwriting differ from narrative or story writing? What made this play so believable to its listeners?

Mystery Madness

Do you like a good mystery? Well, what could appear more mysterious than the comets, planets, and stars? Try using the riddles of space, and the facts you are learning, to write—and solve—a mystery of your own.

 YOU WILL NEED

☐ science mysteries, such as the Einstein Anderson stories
☐ astronomy reference books
☐ a good imagination

 PROCEDURE

1. Read several short mysteries. The Einstein Anderson stories are about a boy who solves problems encountered by his friends and family. After the problem is presented, the reader has a chance to solve the mystery before Einstein reveals his solution. The solution is always based on a scientific fact or principle.

2. Look through several astronomy books, reading for little-known facts or concepts.

3. Using the Einstein Anderson character, or making up one of your own, write a short science mystery that your character is able to solve using a scientific fact or concept.

4. Try to stump your classmates with your mysteries. You may want to allow your readers time to check their astronomy books for a solution.

 DIGGING DEEPER

What's the difference between science fiction and using science *in* fiction? How careful or creative should an author be when using science information?

 IN YOUR JOURNAL

Writing Einstein Anderson stories gave Seymour Simon an opportunity to teach science concepts *and* tell corny jokes. What did you like about writing these mysteries?

 READ MORE ABOUT IT

Compare the Einstein Anderson mysteries to the Encyclopedia Brown stories. How are they the same? How are they different?

 SEYMOUR SAYS

I wrote the Einstein Anderson mysteries when I taught junior high school in New York City. I would write these stories and give them out in class. The kids that solved the mysteries earned the title Einstein for a Day.

I used to tell corny jokes in class, and the students never laughed, so I put all these jokes in the Einstein books and let him tell them.

Survey of the Stars

How much do your friends, family, and teachers know about our Solar System or the universe beyond? Why not survey some of them to see how space smart they really are. You might be surprised by the answers to some easy-looking questions.

 YOU WILL NEED

☐ astronomy books, star atlases, encyclopedias
☐ booklet or bulletin board materials (pencils or markers, paper)

 PROCEDURE

1. Browse through a number of astronomy books, looking for interesting and unusual facts. Make a list of some of the most interesting items you find.

2. Use your list of facts to develop at least ten questions into a space quiz. Here are a few questions to get you started:

Question: *How many planets have rings?*
Note: *Most people think of Saturn when they picture a planet with rings, but there are actually four planets with rings. Use information from* Our Solar System *to identify the ringed planets.*

Question: *What is our closest star?*
Note: *If you said the Sun, you're right. But some people forget that our Sun is actually a star. Look in* Stars *to find out what is the next-nearest star.*

Question: *How many stars other than our Sun have planets orbiting around them?*
Note: *It's hard to believe, but out of the billions of stars in the universe, astronomers have never positively identified a solar system other than our own. Do any exist? Look at the picture of Beta Pictoris in* Stars. *What do you think?*

3. Give your space quiz to several people. Make a graph to keep track of which questions stumped the most people.

4. Find a way to educate your community about astronomy facts. You could publish a booklet, write a column for your school newspaper, hang a factoid bulletin board in your school, or even videotape short infomercials that present fun, and factual, information.

 DIGGING DEEPER

Share and analyze the results of your space quizzes with your classmates.

- What group of quiz takers answered the most questions correctly—students, parents, teachers, or librarians? Why do you think this is so?
- Were there any questions that stumped everyone? No one?
- What could you as a class do to better educate your school community?

 IN YOUR JOURNAL

Is it important that people have the most accurate information about our Solar System and the universe beyond? Why?

 READ MORE ABOUT IT

For really up-to-date information on space, you might be better off looking through magazines, newspapers, and journals. Even if you don't understand every word or concept, enjoy the photographs and captions.

Special astronomy magazines include *Odyssey* (for kids), *Sky & Telescope,* and *Astronomy.* You'll also find more general science magazines, like *Discover,* provide a lot of astronomy coverage.

Many photos of Saturn and its moons were used to create this picture.

 SEYMOUR SAYS

I wrote my first book, Space Monsters, when I was in second grade. I wrote it because I liked reading stories about space monsters.

I made up a trip to a zoo on a distant planet, and I imagined all kinds of animals. I drew the pictures and my teacher stapled it together. Then I read it to the class.

When I grew up, I remembered that book and wrote it again. I still called it Space Monsters, but this time I wrote about all the monsters I'd loved as a kid—the thrilling monsters I'd read about in science-fiction magazines and books and the ones I'd seen in the movies.

Biography Bash

Would Galileo believe his eyes if he saw a picture of Earth from space? Would Columbus believe the discoveries of the twentieth century?

"A picture I really like is one of the most famous photographs of the twentieth century, of the Earth and the Moon. When people first look at it, they think it's a picture from Earth of a moonrise. But actually, it's a picture of an Earthrise as seen from the Moon. We could not see that picture unless it had been taken from the Moon."

—Seymour Simon

 YOU WILL NEED

☐ biographies of scientists and astronomers from books, encyclopedias, videos
☐ astronomy books and magazines with up-to-date information

 PROCEDURE

Throughout the ages, curious women and men have wanted to learn about the Sun, the Moon, the planets, and the stars. Choose a scientist of the past and introduce him or her to the astronomy of the twentieth century.

1. Read about the person's life and scientific interests and discoveries.

2. Learn about the times your person lived in. What did people know and believe about the universe? Did your person agree with these ideas or did she or he have different opinions?

3. Become knowledgeable about your scientist's field.

4. Choose an astronomy book published in the 1990s, and then write a story in which your historical figure travels through time to the twentieth century and discovers that book.

If, for instance, you choose Galileo, you might ask:

- What would he already know about the topic?
- Would he believe what is in the book?
- What misinformation about the topic would he have?
- What would surprise him most about the facts and photos?
- What would he want to know more about?
- What would he want to do next, and where would he want to go?

5. Some of you may want to write this story in reverse. Send a twentieth-century scientist *back* to visit people living in earlier times. Your character can take one book with her.

If, for instance, you choose astronaut Kathryn Sullivan, you might ask:

- What book would she take?
- How would she convince her historical hosts that she was from the twentieth century?
- What would she tell the people about her scientific work?
- What would she tell them about astronomy today?
- What questions do you think the modern scientist would ask? Where would she want to go?

6. Publish and read your story, or produce it as a play or video.

 DIGGING DEEPER

- After the class has shared stories, introduce the various scientists to one another. What would

The landscape of the Moon and a crescent Earth, as seen by Apollo 17 astronauts.

their conversations be about? What would they ask one another?

- Hold a science conference with the historical figures you've met. Who would lead the meetings? What would they be about? What facts could the scientists agree on?

IN YOUR JOURNAL

If you could ask a question of any scientist you met in this activity, what would it be?

READ MORE ABOUT IT

To get you started, here are the names of a few people who have studied the skies above them.

There are many more; see who else you can find.

Aristotle	Caroline Herschel
Benjamin Banneker	William Herschel
Charles Bolden	Hipparchos
Tycho Brahe	Edwin Hubble
Jocelyn Bell Burnell	Johannes Kepler
Annie Jump Cannon	Henrietta Swan Leavitt
Nicolaus Copernicus	Maria Mitchell
Albert Einstein	Isaac Newton
Galileo Galilei	Claudius Ptolemy
William Gilbert	Sally Ride
Edmund Halley	Kathryn Sullivan

Significant contributions were also made by the ancient Chinese, Greeks, Mayans, and people from other ancient cultures.

Looking at Books, Old and New

Shuttle missions, space telescopes—new data is constantly being received, and with new information, books quickly become out-of-date. What's a librarian to do?

Here are some suggestions for updating the materials at your school.

 YOU WILL NEED

☐ books on astronomy, old and new
☐ sources of current information—
  newspapers, TV reports, NASA publications

 PROCEDURE

1. Take a fast survey of the astronomy books in your library and compare their contents with your most up-to-date information.

- You may want to divide the class into groups, assigning each group one topic, such as planets; the Sun; stars and galaxies; comets, meteors, and asteroids; and space travel.
- Record the titles, authors, and publication dates and the accuracy of information of some of the books in your library.
- Report back to the class.

2. Compare your findings with those of your classmates. Were the books of one category more outdated than another? Decide which books in your library need to be updated. Is it only those published before a certain date? Or is it only the ones about certain planets or topics?

3. Devise a plan for updating the books. Here are some suggestions. You may think of others.

- Errata slips. Sometimes publishers discover an error *after* a book has been printed. Rather than reprinting every book, they place an errata slip inside the cover. This form states the location of the error and provides the correct information. You could create a version of this form to make corrections in your books.

- Reference book. Develop a reference binder to be kept at the librarian's desk, listing specific corrections by book title, author, and page number. Borrowers could refer to the reference guide whenever they check an astronomy book out of the library. You'll need to devise a system to tag the books that have corrections in the binder.
- Rewrite. Write a revised mini edition of an out-of-date book and place it on the shelf beside the original. Ask the librarian if you can add it to the card catalog.

 DIGGING DEEPER

It's not only *what* is said that changes; sometimes books differ in *how* the information is presented or how the book looks.

With a partner, find two astronomy books written at least ten years apart. These could be two books by the same author or two books about the same topic. Compare the books by answering these questions:

- Are the facts up-to-date in both books?
- How is the subject matter approached by each author? Humorously? Seriously? Like a textbook? Like a comic book?
- How do the authors talk to the readers?

  ○ Do they state facts, tell a story, ask questions, or write as if they were having a conversation with the reader?
  ○ Do the authors talk down to readers, as if the readers were stupid or very young? Do they give too much information without explanation, as if the readers already knew all the facts?

A solar observatory.

- What is different about the look of the books?

  ○ Are there photos or drawings in each? Is there color?
  ○ Are there a lot of words on the page, or is there plenty of space?
  ○ Is one book easier to read or to handle?

- Which book would you use for pleasure reading? For a report? Recommend to a friend? Why?

Compare your findings with those of others.

 IN YOUR JOURNAL

- What should libraries do with very old books? Are some books so old they are not worth updating, or are all books valuable resources?
- What information that we now understand as fact is most likely to change? Why?

Space Convention

Astronomers and other scientists often attend science meetings and conventions to keep up on the latest science research. You can share your science research and questions by holding a mini convention with your class, grade, or entire school.

 YOU WILL NEED

☐ books, newspaper articles, and other research materials

☐ one or more rooms to set up your convention

 PROCEDURE

1. Set a date for your convention, allowing plenty of time to research and prepare. Make sure it does not interfere with other important events at your school. Send out invitations to students in other classes who might want to attend your convention.

2. Talk to adults who have attended science conventions. Find out what goes on. How do people present their research? How do they debate issues? How do they keep in touch after their convention?

3. As a class, brainstorm a list of research topics, displays, and debates for your convention. Here are some suggestions to start your list:

- an in-depth study of one planet
- space stations—is it possible to sustain life in space for long periods of time?
- terraforming on Mars—can a planet be adapted to support human life?
- comets
- telescopes—optical, infrared, X-ray, and space-based telescopes
- exploration—how is space exploration similar to the early Earth explorations of Columbus, Magellan, and others?
- looking back in time—the mysteries of quasars

4. Make a sign-up sheet for those who would like to present some research.

5. As you plan, you will need to set a schedule of events and decide:

- How long each session should last.
- How many sessions will run at one time.
- How many people can attend each session.

6. The final plans for your convention will need to be suited to your particular class. Use the questions in Digging Deeper to help you organize your day.

 DIGGING DEEPER

What details will make your convention a success? Decide which ones are important to your group and identify who will make sure each one is done.

- Do you want to invite a speaker or special guests—parents, your principal, or a local scientist?
- Do you need publicity in the school or local paper, or through the morning school announcements?
- If students from other classes or other guests are attending, should they have name tags?
- How about designing personal business cards with a logo to represent your topic?
- Do you want special refreshments or souvenirs?
- How are you going to record the event—with photographs, on video, or in an article for the school newspaper?

Some of the planets in the Solar System. Io, Europa, Ganymede, and Callisto are four of Jupiter's moons; Titan is Saturn's largest moon.

In Your Journal

List several reasons why it is important for scientists to get together and discuss their questions, their research, and their concerns.

Read More about It

One way to read about current work or interest in science is via a computer bulletin board. See if a teacher or parent in your school can help you access a local network of kids or adults interested in astronomy.

Seymour Says

If you were to ask what kinds of projects are science projects, my answer to that would be, "I can't think of anything that isn't science." Think about any subject, and I'm willing to bet there is something scientific about it.

The Lunar Olympics

"How about having a scale that shows what you would weigh on the Moon?" Einstein suggested to Margaret. "We can use the balance scale from the school nurse's room. Then we can write the Moon weight figures on cardboard and tape them to the scale."

"That's a good idea," replied Margaret. "We'll just divide each of the weight numbers on the scale by six. That will give us the weights on the Moon."

"Right," said Einstein. "The Moon's gravitational pull is only one-sixth as strong as Earth's. So a person would weigh only one-sixth as much on the Moon as on Earth."

"That's a great way to lose weight," said Margaret. "The only trouble is that your mass remains the same, so that you look the same as you do on Earth."

"Let's review what we have so far for the Lunar Olympics. We have a weight lifting contest, and we'll label the weights with numbers one-sixth of their Earth weight—"

"Won't Pat be happy when he can lift a few hundred pounds over his head!" interrupted Margaret.

"Pat is already so bigheaded that he can't find an aspirin that will fit him," Einstein agreed. "He's always trying to push himself forward by patting himself on the back."

"Don't get started telling jokes," said Margaret. "We have to stage the Lunar Olympics of the year 2100 at Moon Base I for our class next week. That means we have to complete the plans today so we know what materials we'll need."

"The materials better not cost too much," said Einstein. "After all, the Moon itself is only worth a dollar."

"What?" Margaret asked bewilderedly.

"The Moon has four quarters, so it's only worth..."

"Never mind, Einstein! Just get on with the plans."

"Sorry about that. Let me see. Besides the weight lifting, we have a shot put contest. Instead of a heavy iron ball, we'll use a baseball painted gray and labeled with a weight six times as heavy as it really is."

"We can have two contests with the ball," said Margaret, "a distance throw and a height throw. Then we can compare the results with a real shot put contest on Earth."

"Say, if an athlete gets athlete's foot, do you know what an astronaut gets?" Einstein asked.

"I'm sure you'll tell me," said Margaret.

"An astronaut gets mistletoe. Get it? Missile-toe."

"I got it," said Margaret, "but I hope it's not catching."

"I wish you'd stop joking around." Einstein laughed. "You're making me into a moon insect—a lunatic. A *lunar tick*. Why aren't you laughing, Margaret?"

"Just get on with it, Einstein," Margaret said, trying to keep from smiling. "Suppose we have a walking race over a hundred-yard course. Only we'll really make the course sixteen yards long. Then we can have a high jump bar labeled six times higher than it really is."

"That's not what would happen on the real Moon, Margaret," said Einstein.

"Are you still joking?" asked Margaret. "If you can throw a weight six times as high and six times as far on the Moon as you can on Earth, then you should be able to walk six times as fast and jump six times as high as you can on Earth."

"This is no joke," said Einstein. "Although it seems logical, it really isn't."

Can you solve the puzzle: Why can't you walk six times faster and jump six times higher on the Moon?

"You'll have to explain that," said Margaret.

"Right," said Einstein. "You see, when you walk on Earth, your body is raised up about one and a half inches with each step. But on the Moon it will drop back more slowly than it does on Earth. On the Moon you would be walking more slowly than you could walk on Earth."

"I think I understand," Margaret said slowly. "But surely a high jumper could jump over a bar six times higher on the Moon."

"He could jump over a higher bar, but not six times higher," said Einstein. "The reason has to do with the way he lifts his feet and where his center of gravity is. Let's say that a high jumper is six feet tall. His center of gravity, the point where all his weight is concentrated, is about three and a half feet off the ground. To jump over a six-foot bar, he has to raise his center of gravity only two and a half feet. To clear the bar, he lifts his legs as far up as possible. That means that he really raised his center of gravity only two and a half feet to jump over the six-foot bar. So on the Moon he wouldn't be able to jump over a thirty-six-foot-high bar."

"How high could he jump?" asked Margaret.

"He could jump six times the two and a half feet, about fifteen feet high. Then if he raised his legs upward the same as on Earth, he could clear another three and a half feet."

"That means he should be able to jump over a bar about eighteen and a half feet high," Margaret calculated. "That's still a pretty good jump."

"Oh, that's not so good," said Einstein. "I bet you I could jump across the room."

"Let's see you do it," said Margaret.

Einstein walked to the other side of the room and then jumped. "I told you I could jump across the room," he said.

Student Bibliography

It would be impossible to write a bibliography of children's astronomy books that lists the best titles for any one classroom, any one reader. As space probes and powerful telescopes collect new data about the planets, stars, and the universe, even the most recent texts rapidly become less than up-to-date. Add the fact that library collections vary, and the concept of a complete list accessible to all becomes very difficult to accomplish.

With that in mind, we offer the titles of Seymour Simon's astronomy books and the titles of recent award-winning books. But do not limit yourself to these titles.

Browse through the astronomy section of *your* library and find books that interest you. Check out the books on either side of the ones you like; find new titles by authors with whom you are familiar; search through the bibliographies in each new book. And don't be afraid to investigate books in the adult section of the library. Astronomy is for everyone. Happy reading!

Astronomy Books by Seymour Simon

Comets, Meteors, and Asteroids. New York: Morrow, 1994

Earth: Our Planet in Space. New York: Four Winds/ Macmillan, 1984

Einstein Anderson Goes to Bat. New York: Puffin, 1987

Einstein Anderson Lights Up the Sky. New York: Puffin, 1987

Einstein Anderson Makes Up for Lost Time. New York: Puffin, 1987

Einstein Anderson, Science Sleuth. New York: Puffin, 1986

Einstein Anderson Sees Through the Invisible Man. New York: Puffin, 1987

Einstein Anderson Shocks His Friends. New York: Puffin, 1986

Einstein Anderson Tells a Comet's Tale. New York: Puffin, 1987

Galaxies. New York: Morrow, 1988

How to Be a Space Scientist in Your Own Home. New York: Lippincott, 1982

Jupiter. New York: Morrow, 1985

Long Journey from Space. New York: Crown, 1982

Long View into Space. New York: Crown, 1979

Look to the Night Sky. New York: Puffin, 1979

Mars. New York: Morrow, 1989

Mercury. New York: Morrow, 1992

The Moon. New York: Four Winds/Macmillan, 1984

Neptune. New York: Morrow, 1991

Our Solar System. New York: Morrow, 1992

Saturn. New York: Morrow, 1985

Space Words. New York: HarperCollins, 1991

Stars. New York: Morrow, 1986

The Sun. New York: Morrow, 1986

Uranus. New York: Morrow, 1987

Venus. New York: Morrow, 1992

Recent Astronomy Titles from the Outstanding Science Trade Books for Children list (NSTA-CBC)

1993

The Visual Dictionary of the Earth. Martyn Bramwell. New York: Dorling Kindersley

The Visual Dictionary of the Universe. Sue Becklake. New York: Dorling Kindersley

1992

Galileo. Leonard Everett Fisher. New York: Macmillan

Galileo and the Universe. Steve Parker. New York: HarperCollins

Our Solar System. Seymour Simon. New York: Morrow

Venus. Seymour Simon. New York: Morrow

Voyager: An Adventure to the Edge of the Solar System. Sally Ride and Tam O'Shaughnessy. New York: Crown

1991

Neptune. Seymour Simon. New York: Morrow

Voyager to the Planets. Necia H. Apfel. New York: Clarion

1990

The Christmas Sky. Franklyn Branley. New York: Crowell

The Great Voyager Adventure: A Guided Tour Through the Solar System. Alan Harris and Paul Weissman. New York: Messner

How Did We Find Out about Neptune? Isaac Asimov. New York: Walker

Small Worlds: Exploring the 60 Moons of Our Solar System. Joseph W. Kelch. New York: Messner

1989

The Big Dipper and You. E. C. Krupp. New York: Morrow

Junk in Space. Richard Haurer. New York: Simon & Schuster

Voyagers from Space: Meteors and Meteorites. Patricia Lauber. New York: Crowell

1988

Galaxies. Seymour Simon. New York: Morrow

The Glow-in-the-Dark Night Sky Book. Clint Hatchett. New York: Random House

I Want to Be an Astronaut. Byron Barton. New York: Crowell

Nebulae: The Birth and Death of Stars. Necia H. Apfel. New York: Lothrop

The Origin and Evolution of Our Own Particular Universe. David E. Fisher. New York: Atheneum

Stars and Planets. Christopher Lampton. New York: Doubleday

UFOs, ETs and Visitors from Space. Melvin Berger. New York: Putnam

U.S. and Soviet Space Programs: A Comparison. David E. Newton. New York: Watts

Classroom Resources

Activity Books
Gardner, Robert. *Projects in Space Science.* New York: Messner, 1988

McKay, David W., and Bruce G. Smith. *Space Science Projects for Young Scientists.* New York: Watts, 1986

Moeschl, Richard. *Exploring the Sky: Projects for Beginning Astronomers.* Chicago: Chicago Review Press, 1989

Schaaf, Fred. *Seeing the Sky: One Hundred Projects, Activities, & Explorations in Astronomy.* New York: Wiley, 1990

Schatz, Dennis. *Astronomy Activity Book.* New York: Little Simon, 1991

There are a number of organizations designed to provide educational resources, programs, and opportunities for students and educators, including:

Challenger Center for Space Science Education
The Challenger Center was founded by the families of the seven crew members of the space shuttle *Challenger.* The center's mission is to teach, explore, and inspire. The center includes high-tech space simulators, located in science centers, museums, school districts, and universities across the United States and Canada; teacher workshops; and international, interactive live teleconferences.

For more information, contact:
>Challenger Center for Space Science Education
>1055 North Fairfax Street, Suite 100
>Alexandria, Virginia 22314
>(703) 683-9740

Young Astronaut Council
Six thousand students participate in the Young Astronaut Program internationally. The Young Astronaut Council is a flexible program designed to provide hands-on space-related activities for the student to do in his or her home, youth group, or school.

For more information, contact:
>Young Astronaut Council
>1308 Nineteenth Street, N.W.
>Washington, D.C. 20036
>(202) 682-1984

NASA Programs
NASA offers a variety of educational programs, including:

- Aerospace Education Services Program (AESP), which conducts workshops for educators and students.
- NASA Educational Workshops for Elementary School Teachers (NEWEST) for grades K–6 teachers and NASA Educational Workshops for Math, Science and Technology Teachers (NEWMAST) for grades 7–12: two-week summer workshops at NASA Field Centers, where educators can interact with NASA scientists and engineers.
- The Space Science Student Involvement Program (SSIP), a nationwide program for children in grades 3 through 12 that builds on art, journalism, and the sciences.
- Nine NASA Teacher Resource Centers (TRCs), located across the United States. They will supply teachers' publications, videotapes, slides, computer programs, and instructional activities.

For more information on these and other NASA programs, contact:
>NASA
>Code FEE
>300 E Street, S.W.
>Washington, D.C. 20546
>202-358-1110

NASA Spacelink is a computer information service for educators and students that provides current news about NASA missions and programs. Spacelink is available via modem (205-895-0028) or through the Internet at spacelink.msfc.nasa.gov.

Project SPICA
Project SPICA (Support Program for Instructional Competency in Astronomy) is a National Science Foundation–funded program operated out of Harvard University/Smithsonian Institution's Center for Astrophysics. Through intensive workshops the program trains master teachers, who in turn serve as astronomy-teaching resource agents. The center has hundreds of teacher-tested activities.

For further information, contact:
>SPICA
>Center for Astrophysics
>60 Garden Street, MS 71
>Cambridge, Massachusetts 02138
>617-495-9798

Resources and Publications for Teachers and Students

AIMS Educational Foundation
P.O. Box 8120
Fresno, California 93747
209-255-4094

Astronomy Magazine
21027 Crossroads Circle
P.O. Box 1612
Waukesha, Wisconsin 53187
414-796-8776

Earth in Space
American Geophysical Union
2000 Florida Avenue, N.W.
Washington, D.C. 20009
202-462-6903

Mercury Magazine
"The Universe in the Classroom" (teacher newsletter)
Astronomical Society of the Pacific
390 Ashton Avenue
San Francisco, California 94112
415-337-1100

Odyssey
Cobblestone Publishing
7 School Street
Peterborough, New Hampshire 03458
603-924-7209

Sky & Telescope
Sky Publishing Corporation
P.O. Box 9111
Belmont, Massachusetts 02178-9111
617-864-7360

Scienceland
501 Fifth Avenue, Suite 2108
New York, New York 10017
212-490-2180

Science World
Scholastic Inc.
555 Broadway
New York, New York 10012
212-343-6100

Sky Calendar
Dept. GT
Abrams Planetarium
Michigan State University
East Lansing, Michigan 48824
517-355-4676

Star Date
University of Texas
McDonald Observatory
RLM 15.308
Austin, Texas 78712
512-471-5285

3-2-1 Contact
Children's Television Workshop
One Lincoln Plaza
New York, New York 10023
212-595-3456

Wonder Science
American Chemical Society
1155 Sixteenth Street, N.W.
Washington, D.C. 20036
202-872-4600

Index